RESTORATION DAY

*

by

HENRY GOULD

ISBN : 978-1-387-63563-4

RESTORATION DAY

TABLE OF CONTENTS

PART ONE

1

This dangle of two-tone tulips in a bright tin can
Nancy Hart painted, once upon a time
in Providence, long ago.
Now a new bunch from the grocery store
shines on the tabletop, like a box of crayons –
so many pale colors (still tulips, all of them).

& Samuel Barber is on the radio (*Violin
Concerto #14*). These frail
harmonic tentacles rise, a bread crust
out of February ice, my bookshelf dust
like drifting puffs of breath over the din
from our defective, splintered capital

& *tomorrow is Valentine's Day*, keens pretty
Ophelia – & *I a maid at your window*.
By Cock, they are to blame.
The sonic synthesis our frames
unframes; the windblown rose will grow
from one soft prison syllable. *Love* (merrily).

2.13.21

2

to F.T.

Late afternoon, one icebox Minnesota day.
I fell asleep on the couch. Sunlight
molts to blazoned air, soldering snow.
I dreamt about you... that you
married, anew. *Anchors aweigh*. Checkmate,
mio cuore. & Sophie brought me this to show :

an ancient blue-green paper toy box
you must have bought by Lake Superior
chock-full of puzzle-blocks in bright color
– scenes of picturesque Duluth (old *signs*

that mock me). Those unglued tiles
my mother firmly molded, long ago –
just you & me, blissfully afloat
above green North Shore granite (not
too far from Gooseberry Falls). My mood
turns deep ice-cold & blue (myself to know).

2.14.21

3

i.m. I.M. Singer

No man is a Rhode Island unto himself,
Henry. Outside your deliquescent &
quiescent states, way past your past,
goodness is infinitely vast –
beyond conjectures, human or elf.
So Nicholas of Cusa would propound

with iridescent intellectual hilarity
(quadrivial, Boethian). So I would be
a singer as Isadore "Is" Singer was,
O Manuel – enfolding fiber bundles
into elastic bridgework... twisty Thierry
Units... harmonious Pythagorean equality!

Meanwhile the presiding spirit of these states
on President's Day as every day
will shed unfathomably providential
free benevolence – perpetual fount
of each voluminous & pirouetting Milky Way;
magnanimous inkling of our common fate.

2.15.21

4

These delicate paper boxes from Boxborough
were *Zhen Xian Bao* (made for holding yarns).
The intricate folds uncrease each other, so –
Sheep's Clothing would have crowned such turns

with special praise. O the secret places

of the universe! Deep crimson rose (lost kisses
in the sky). You must walk the woodland path
alone, at dusk... until you fuse these matrices
of *one & many* – solitary flight, familiar nest.

2.15.21

10

5

What would be the point of having a priest
dab a spot of ash on your forehead,
sparrow? Heart's deep distress
for restoration, born of otherness.
Your special providence, facing toward East
to join the general Jubilee... rise from the dead...

So the *King of Paradise* might come again
lifting the rusted piers, the broken bulwarks.
Branching like inimitable Nicholas of Cusa –
persistent, indefatigable Odysseus
ever-glorifying his sweet *Father of Sparks*
(imminent & omnipresent *O*, beyond our ken).

& the heart comes home, like those tulips
in the icon. Back to her Providence
sleeping underneath its beautiful books.
Like Nicholas too, back to his nooks –
where an instinct of passionate sentience
calls him to Galilee. To one elliptical eclipse.

2.17.21

6

That one might hold opposing points in equilibrium
in order to form a more perfect idiot
was a project for Nicholas of Cusa (bright
genial advocate of elegant proof). Animal awe
evokes a mathematical continuum
& oneness underwrites presence of intellect

(i.e., your mind). *Ergo*, God might exist.
& hope's a theological virtue, Henry –
for each retired librarian in musty cell
engraved by plague (parochial hell).
That bird's-eye view by Maxwell Mays
of green, elusive Providence... communalist

New England riverbay! Nostalgia kitsch,
no doubt. Yet hope's an irrepressible dream...
beauty both lure & anchor. Which is witch?
Leo's *Vitruvian Man* – both groin & starry beam.

2.18.21

7

This splashy tulip spray for Valentine' Day –
transparent vase of yellows & pinks, maroon
& mauve – already puffed & drooping now.
A valediction for their own swift undertow.
Circuiting my *Game of Spheres* (bright play
of flippant waves with anchor's plummet line).

Graceful Providence floats in my hazy cloud
of old regrets & enervated memories. Yet
ripples radiate from Roger Williams' well –
one moss-green Lincoln penny, out of hell
hums to evening's western rim. Earth-shroud
for tears' gaze (smiling through melting net).

When the *Perfect* comes, the *Eternal* comes –
as Oscar Cullmann says, *when the Redemption
that has already happened shines in the world*
(& in your mind) it will be that mother-of-pearl
thread of silver, shuttle-crossing the loom's
keel, like a scallop-shell... your palm's glowing sun.

2.19.21

8

Today the light snow shapes a soft *andante*.
Brownian motion, like a floating world
through twilight afternoon. Aimlessly
adrift, in adoration, toward the crevasse
of the Mississippi, as the river hurls south
& quarries straight down (obstinate ass).

Love being a force in the *Unified Field*
like gravity or magnetism – transcending,
superseding the flow of clocktime. One
beloved face, coppery, minted on stone.
The riverbed sleeps beneath her shield
of flowing bronze (Sophie's mane, unending).

So I open the little paper box of memories,
like a seashell casket, or *Vierge Ouvrante*.
Frail mandorla in the mirror, or canoe.
Rhode Island is this flinty *imago* of you –
salt mewl of *Lady Liberty* (mild, adamant).
Feminine cosmos... rose tent of calm seas.

2.21.21

9

to Andy Lapham

What if Paradise is near, occluded somewhere
in your damaged soul? & heaven be the dream
of simple salty multitudes – their chaste
familial tomorrows? This lonely Adam's quest
(this Andrew Everyman). To share a permaculture
farm, in "gritty" central Minneapolis – *mon áme,*

mon frère... a relic of high-hearted Providence!
Your *grave Sienese profile*, Francesca. The
tiny forest-green farmhouse, corner of 6th
(132). Theodicy of blind headstrong Odysseus...

Beatrice is a "9" (*madonna primum mobile*).
A light through one canoe-cocoon
(limbs' equal joy). My origami rose,
more plain & true than you suppose –
more lasting than your iron ferris wheel.
Her peony, her acorn prince, is coming soon.

2.22.21

10

The sky at dusk, after sundown (looking
southwest). Washed by darkness,
barely. Pale rose where the sun was.
Anemic royal blue. Stillness
(old wooden family kitchen). Reckoning
the near-immeasurable rising of Venus,

accompanied by galactic entourage
(blithe, fiery, faint). Such an awkward
concert of opposites, this marriage
of contrarieties! Like *middle age* &
modern youth. Like Nicholas, the papal sage
& Roger, puritan separatist... who shared

the soft whisper of a far transcendence –
brace-embracing, inconceivable sun!
Only tolerance & human dignity
will reconcile pride & humility,
Union & *Liberty*; only Rhode Island insolence
could instaurate the root of Paradise (American).

2.25.21

11

Paradise. A bend of shoreline north of Newport
bent out of sand and puddingstone
to origami seagull. Meticulous report
sent by LaFarge. One sheep, asleep, in sunlit zone;

one sailor's salt Pacific yarn (spun to Japan).

Clover, in stained glass. For Henry Adams?
You taught me the meaning of *shibui.*
Not *ukiyo-e,* rather *shibui.* For free. Love
shatters coral chains... drowns pleasure-domes.

2.28.21

12

This year, March tripped in like a lamb.
A frosty understatement. Linen gift
outright. *Power, power all the way*
enthuses effervescent JFK...
such as we were, she was, I am (*a hey
ey-yo*). Such violence. Heart skips (adrift).

The old gnarled poet in the dead forest
leans against an oak, predicts an almond
grace. A restoration of the child,
whose adoration, meek & mild
is etched (with adequate abjection) by the best
rail-splitter in our copious realm (mute *demi-monde*).

& if we want to wake up from this nightmare,
Nicholas of Kues (who left his heart there
saved by a Jew from MI6) offers a path –
unperfect actor, wobbling through wrath
(so slowly, slowly) back to Ithaka. To love,
to share. Plain wooden bowl (beyond compare).

3.1.21

13

The poem ruffles sails... a whiff of sea-air
mingled with spring mildness. Salt
& clover. For the invalid, the prisoner
clamped in stale walls. Your sprightly mother
with her earthen herbs. *America*, for Walt.
Nobody's fault if little Rhody's hardly there.

The baby of the Colonies, the first & last (13th).
With glittery blade in the Triangle Trade
(rum, cotton, human grief) – still full
of ailments, provincial, colonial, parochial.
While blithe sea-roses nod along that enfilade
of rock & azure, hemming in sweet Williams' plinth.

Your place in history is not assured, my rude
& ruddy rudder-rood. Glum mechanics
of infinite May impugn the Federal Triangle
with sniper's mangonel & mangle;
so sell some clamshell coins for your seafood –
one Penny Arcade redeems Broadways, Boardwalks.

3.3.21

14

A year & a year, like sphere with sphere
overlapping one cubic hexagon. A single
flashing snowflake. Like tiny silver
quahog coffin, or barnacled Viking bier.
Your transcendental number curves near,
dear one – your gaze alights my soul's ingle.

That sonorous sound of the infinite seashore
scrapes like a fiddlehead crab, beneath.
Flinty as obdurate Roger, Thomas More –
for love blazes like innocence, pure sheath

of fire. You sense that potentiality
in the deep shadow, the remote forest
of your own childhood – among those golden
kindly books, sweet planetary imagination...
With malice toward none, with charity
for all (chaste rosy throne in thorny nest).

3.4.21

15

Robin will yodel for the archaic poet posthumous
working outside from his plastic throne, this day
so infinitely mild (past each & all frostbitten march
in memory). Use *infinite* advisedly. These porch
steps, one-by-one, down to heart's fathomless...
Obscurity blurs rose V (proceed to point [P]).

Henry's potentiality, or impotential, is implicit
in each poem's tensile, uncomfortable
prong (unconfidential). So Little Rhody
folds (via reciprocal equation) the broody
vastness of an *Ocean State.* Mind her unstable
pebbly mosaic. How to reclaim yon guileless wit,

Robin's unforced, incalculable innocence?
How shalt thy Psalter be restored? The song
that Cantor sings, & Singer hums – the child's
Aleph, Leontyne's Nazorean Samuel chords...
Humility is limitless. & Ithaka is Providence,
immovable – threading her right from wrong.

3.8.21

16

If in March the primavera breeze picks up
a rushing freight train through the forlorn yards
like some transparent serpent of the nation
hungry for power (as revenge or consolation) –
then this evanescent wind-chime earns its keep,
sounds four tendrilous bronze pipes (beyond words).

Its coppery spiral, like a figurehead (some
penny carving of one suffering wight – so brave,
wise & humane) is Liberty's untarnished idiom –
riddle of an unplumbed Union, risen from the grave.

In the wild marshland south of Galilee
shards of buried & forgotten bones
are glued & welded like an icon, or a wave
mosaic in Byzantium. One salient architrave.
Union, equality, connection... these lasting three
meld into octaves for Agee (Samuel's bell-tones).

3.9.21

17

O Lord, my fumbly bumblings, to communicate!
Here, at the crossroads of the middle waist,
by St. Tonius Berryman Falls – amidships,
nigh found'ring good ol' *Constitution* [nips
from hipflask]... & where Herman now, our best?
O salty bros & sisses of the soil... cornfused by hate!

The Reason of the nominal empiricists, &/or
empirical nominalists, hath improved
not much. *Mind the door*, crowed Milton.
&, as with Philo, reckoned that razor line
dividin' dove fro dove, & men from *Elohim* (sore
whiners). His fren' Wms. spake Narragansett; loved.

& as with jovial imperturbable St. Nicholas,
they carried each other, sans care – the same
& the otter, the red black n' white, the hitman, the
whoman... O bird-bright, afro-paradisiac dreamland!
Sheba herself from Yemen, Ethiopia, no less –
her *One* brought *Union* & *Equality* (chaste flame).

3.10.21

18

They return your gaze from the old photograph,
these people, standing near your whole life long.
Sad unfazed Florence, with her plangent laugh.
Two bully uncles, off to hold Bastogne.

& two teased favorites (unruffled John, Mary).

One crimson yarn, like Woodpecker's crown
enfolds triangulated magnitudes, irrational
yearning. Federal t-square, Ferrara twin-canoe.
Rahab's hint, & Ariadne's clue. Love trues it all.

3.11.21

19

As the poet shapes up worlds from mumbling
so intellect of *Wakan Tanka*, Holy Ghost
unfolds a universe – woven so seamlessly
none may divide dream from reality.
& when I recollect my fractured, fumbling
kaleidoscope... I measure Providence the most.

I see it there, its granite grey & buff limestone
unsure, bashful, beneath a sweeping ocean rain.
Rotating (*shibui*) with origami symmetry
like some brush-stroke of *Black Ship* poetry
from Federal Hill, near Dante Street... by Fones
Alley... over to Fox Point (where our walks began).

The nation's lit with pyrotechnical articulations
spun by glamor & necessity – the violence
of dynamos, the vagrant shadow of Ophelia's
heart. So I imprint your sandy salience,
a horseshoe liberty of useless sighs.
Blue salt Atlantic floor; rose-hip vibrations.

3.12.21

20

Henry, perhaps you're pondering infinity these days
because your own timeline's grown undeniably
curtailed – inverse, that is. *Merci.* Sure, Bones.
& long-gone reels of careless wastrel drones
with sweet clear eddies of Arcadian kid-plays
are dust of infinitesimal *discontinua*, apparently...

– Some Samsonite saloon Rhodialin' cutting floor?
Please, man. Spin Transcendental B's frisbees.
Hard Knocksville, summer 2015. I want to hear
Leontyne, lady – Marian, beneath the joe-pye trees.

Sheba benign, whorled in bare cube coccoon.
My quiet & astute father, 'mid groaning spring
lifted one index from his deathbed toward the sky
& drew a slow soft circle there. Goodbye, goodbye.
I want to join that congregation, Butch... croon
cowboy songs with all my friends, one sweet morning.

3.14.21

21

The freight trains trundle, careful & slow, across.
The railroad bridge spans a night river – the
Mississippi, silent serpent, always moving.
We are far from Providence here. Roving
Miantonomi, on *path P*, mapped his own *YHWH*
to please R. Wms (restless exile, full of wave-toss).

& youngster Williams sought to please Sir Edw. Coke,
his legal master in the great regal world –
of crown & gown, of sudden axe & interested
speech. The jungle of the blessed, blistered
fang (divine impunity, coiled power's ermine cloak).
Heart flickers in obscurity – a cowrie (sealed, pearled).

Canonicus & Miantonomi... a new protectorate.
He studies their peacekeeping means – solving
extremities of dowry shells, disputed grounds;
primordial fairness, by such reasonable sounds
reminds him of Coke's common root (the *right
of every Englishman*). Plain human dignity I sing.

3.14.21

22

These late snowflakes, in their multitudes
angling down at the center of Lent, on the cusp
of Spring. They bring to mind St. Valentine,
enfolding his *lettere* secreted from prison
& Nicholas, wayfaring bookman bishop
opening beryllium enfoldments of beatitudes.

Your microcosm might be Providence! they cry.
Junk jewelry capital? Absolute rotundity?
Nay, somewhere in between. On an arc
with Melville's cycloid universal iridium track
(hermetic, certainly). Cosmoperfect symmetry
uncoils, with evanescent things, perpetual *Home Ec*.

The north star of the North Star sits beyond
our ken. But listen to the merciful refrain
of Lincoln's murmurous Inaugural; behold
the soulful image on each copper coin. Mild
Old Abe. A servant (from the plain woodland).
One self-effacing face – one silver-penny hexagon.

3.15.21

23

We never danced, we never kissed; we strove
side-by-side, in that abandoned factory, for years
& years. You were a sea-cat in your cove,

Ellen Ryan – casting a chill glance on thick senators,
thin lawyers, sniffing round the State House;
we were JFK's sly lambs (the VISTA volunteers).

Faint echoes from the Patrick's Day parades
down Smith Street, past the pastel tenements,
the capitol dome. Faint scent of April innocence,
ma chère – your heart's devotion never fades.

Like that tiny cube of salt, unbreakable, drifting
in a raindrop from your eye, toward the sea;
communion of the common good goes sifting,

even now, sheep from the goats. & melancholy
mingles with my joy, when fiddlers ring –
the quatrefoils of Kennedys, life's sweet folly.

3.23.21

24

Spring, spring. Streaks in on steady pulse
across the bare flatlands, brash breeze.
Streams in on clear air. Dogs bark.
Chickadees waft their wistful ark
(*Sea-Bee*, *Sea-Bee*) across windowsills.
Now smallest, lowest, poorest things... unfreeze.

The infinitesimal minimum declares its rule.
A figment the size of Rhode Island
without male or female, slave or free
sounds plausible to me – that lone oak tree
where winsome Charlie hid for a day (its bole
an acorn throne) is odd enough to understand.

Everything American recasts its wintry parts.
The wellspring curls into its opposite,
the tiniest droplet into *Ocean State*.
Love, giving way, makes hate evaporate.
Jackie & Jack somehow resuscitate the arts –
Hamlet... Ophelia... to rose & clover knit.

3.20.21

25

The woodpecker priest pried honeybees, honey
from a hollow holm oak. He sanded his memory
through 15 unseen worlds – like Hagiwara, Hideo
hidden behind austere, rectangular Mt. Fuji (*hey*

ey yo). So Providence flickers her kaleidoscope

of contrary confessions... a mirror-bright lake,
a twilit dream. The granite sand's still grey.
The stars are everywhere the same. She'll make
a poncho like gold honey; you will wear one day.

3.22.21

26

Snow was falling generally... sextillions
of minute hexagons. Just yesterday. *It
took 18 months to build the damn thing*, sd
the snowflake master, Dr. Myhrvold.
& this is *Lady Day*, *in Lent* – annunciations
everywhere (circumference a zigzag circuit).

The Shigir Idol is a 9-foot totem pole.
Oldest mobiliary artwork ever found.
Eight faces, geometric tattoos. Two lips,
open-mouthed – to chant, or scream. Chips
ricochet from honey-rings of larch (hole-
peck by pileated Scythian). Gold burial mound.

I don't know how to say it, but your face
emerging from these hair-thin threads
& myriad pebble-tesserae, looks back at me.
Your smile engraves some simultaneity
no galaxy enfolds. So snowflakes trace
love's lost seacoast – hearts' empty beds.

3.25.21

27

This lovely photograph, so flat & still.
My parents, John & Mary, married today
70 years ago – smiling, arms extended
to each other's shoulders (like a mended
H). Byzantium was built on such a triple
cubic incarnation (mourning's anniversary).

Early spring rain, an unobtrusive mist.
All our dogma's grown from simple seeds
of grief. Yet Love will not insist – she is
dislodged *Ecclesia* (surrender's deeds).

Tomorrow is Palm Sunday. My low king
will catch the shuttle to Jerusalem
& kids will lift green fronds between
the pews. Providence remains unseen.
Blind poets suture treads of everything.
The choir above... our unison is up to them.

3.27.21

28

Sometimes a painting stirs embers of memory.
That midwestern farmyard, in deep twilight,
under an elm tree, by the kitchen door.
Sea-dog Verrazano spied, hove-to in 1524
an Island in the form of a triangle (writ he)
about the size of the Isle of Rhodes... quite

lovely, too. Will be dubbed *Ocean State*
one day. & where is the heart of the sea?
Where is that rose, harbored over its hearth
in the human soul? The hero of the Earth,
gentle *Adonai-Adonis...* whose checkmate
of the Minotaur spends out his own mortality?

Love is a mode of invisible fire, that builds,
never destroys – stronger than death,
stronger in the soul than steel or bronze.
As Magdalen dashed through the gardens
so the human heart responds – her fancy gilds
the lamps of dusk with infant dreams (soft breath).

3.28.21

29

i.m. Anny Ballardini

See how the golden threads on the weaver's frame
glow with the rosy warmth of your swift palm
shuttling invisibly above the booming brace.
Mint sheepfold, clover microcosm – my disgrace!
Colossus of Rhodes, archive of borrowed fame...
drowsy librarian, envious scribe... your deathly calm!

For Dante, weakness curled into eternal flame.
Love called with shrill commanding cry
& Italy kindled anew – the blacksmith
hammered out his copper shield of truth.
Virgo's baton, Athena's helm... (Demeter's claim);
Venusian refining fire; free spark – soul-firefly!

& on this small snow-globe, this green island
your fife rings over my sluggish *accidia*
like someone weaving a Bayeux romance.
The lighted circle of loving intelligence
these ladies I betrayed will dance, tri-ribboned
band, for Ariadne... (ancient chaste enigma).

3.29.21

30

Today, Hong Kong. Beijing crops April blossoms.
Three old fools (of press, of unions, & of law)
shipped off to labor camp – to polish the facade
of Machiavellian overlords (gulling the crowd).
Monotony of sameness frames their sums.
And flowers wilt, processed in power's craw.

That lofty cliffside porch in Providence
where Williams gazes toward the western sun.
Rose granite quiddity... Roger's bright insolence.
What cheer, Netop – wellspring's invention?

Soul-flash of transplanetary LOVE
is as the blue cones in Lake Baikal depths.
Cherenkov radiation – Domogatski's lodestar
morphs him into his own neutrino. *For
it, the universe is a transparent world.* High above,
below, within... a chaste equality (cosmic precepts).

4.1.21

31

That I carry around faint tones of memories
whose fleeting presence (at the edge of vision)
like a kid's intuition of some graver realm
or like a ball-toss in Cusa's *pelota* game
means more to me than all my victories
in love & war (insipid bookworm's indecision).

On Easter Day the great kenotic shades
lift up their pink palm-fans of faithfulness.
The fortitude of M.L. King in Memphis
chanting prophetic elegiac hopefulness
rhymes with the monarch butterfly cascades
rising from cedars, into everlastingness.

Today the encrypted figures in my heart
cluster around some Chartres labyrinth
where Ariadne mingles with Penelope.
That golden thread you warped for me
once, long ago, in Providence... cut short.
Only six seraph wings can mend our seventh.

4.4.21

32

When I am old, & waiting for the rain
leaning against a sunny wall in Providence
half a century ago... I murmur it back again.

Prince Roger in his ecstasy will dance
his upstart epileptic glee – rose
dignity of human liberty, all his parlance.

& you, Ophelia-Penelope. Your kayak (*3-x-3*)
goes singing, thinking. So your reign
might crack adamant Ithaka – by charity.

4.5.21

33

Spring buffalo thunder across the sky
following each flash of riverine lightning.
My neighbor Mura hikes along the sidewalk
his cotton sweatband against wind & rain.
We mutter words along separate trails.
Perhaps melodies unite, at the vanishing point.

Minneapolis to Providence is one plane flight
yet Roger seems a fiery Christopher-Charon.
A psychopomp, translating cloudy *Dioscuri*
(sacred & civic, holy & profane). Bright talk
of Madison... witty glamor of Jefferson... stung
with the lash, deformed by sword (split rails).

We wrestle words as carpenters pound nails.
Yet poetry? Not worth a copper mite.
A hungry orphan traces something glowing
with the power of the king – the people's cry;
Coke's lawbook – like a score for violin;
union of *way truth life*... (circles the block).

4.6.21

34
wherein the poet's granddaughter plans
a Suzuki recital with "unicorn" theme

In Susan's house, on Savoy Street, across
from Redeemer's medieval shade – the old
people's church (offering the first free pews
in Providence). Peeking down stairs
from a western wall... on green bed of moss,
beneath round apple tree, at rest... behold

a woven unicorn. Not Cloisters cast-off
but a young girl's fancy – warped on a loom
in Lewiston, long time ago. By Susan's friend
(& Sophie's grandmother). Each art work's end
a quiddity, inimitable & unforeseen – even gruff
maestro will admit the same (it frames his doom).

Every figure is an end, as each equality of one
rests in the shade of love's innumerable One.
Rhode Island is not quite an island (as one Donne
reminds) – so Sophie's recital crowns a unison.

4.7.21

35

That little forest-green farmhouse we found
in the Summit neighborhood, down the block
from Miriam Hospital. You still live there.
Quiet thunder of the loom. A Sabbath air.
A *jeu d'esprit* by Maxwell Mays – not profound
Providence, but Newport Paradise (pink chalk).

The salt scrapes out a pearl under the sea,
slowly – the way Boethius awaits *Lady Philosophy*
or the Interrogator. Patiently (stoic, flickering).
His chaos & necessity, enfolded, like a humming
in the mind, branch into Nikolai's equality – an
equilibrium of oakleaf shade. Pushkinian harmony.

& Thierry at Chartres, Nicholas at his last Kues
balance their acorns on a vanishing point
like circus doctors of theology, like some Fellini
yodeling Roma or Ferrara (by the Black Sea).
The tides of Providence... no one can choose,
whose rocky rhythm only moonlight may anoint.

4.8.21

36

for the persecuted of Xinjïang

Observe how the fatalism of domination works
relentlessly for control. Through avarice &
vanity, through pride & fear... the violence
of despair. So the *Party of the People* spins
atop flexible dogmas of money & perks –
always seeking that equilibrium (a stable brand).

& the fist must rule. Power must concentrate
in the charismatic figurehead – for its moment
of personal apotheosis (communal euphoria).

April is the month of my neighbor's forsythia.
Its yellow-gold petals floresce... a small incarnate
sun (like that smoking bush, muttering unspent).

& I remember her April twin, in Providence.
That blithe witch hazel, climbing over the wall
by the Spanish House (on Prospect Street) –
divining rod against inertia, time's bittersweet
seasons. The ineffable, exalted shepherd of all
is your self-effacing servant (love's intelligence).

4.10.21

37

i.m. John D. and Mary A. Gould

You were the youngest of three brothers, & she
was your twin sister, & today would be
your birthdays. Here, in the old neighborhood
under a misty April rain (by the southbound road
of the broad river-snake, brown Mississippi).
As time's slow circling brings it all back to me.

How the *sister-dove* planted a feminine seed
for the twin children, in the Twin Cities.
Your vulnerable reserve, your gentleness.
Young magnolias (rapture from crushing need).

The life of the soul (that introspective monk's
ecstatic intellect propounds) is softest whispers
of a spring, a sweet fountain; is like a seed
unfolding through each vein, a golden mead
up to its *Restoration Day*. These riverbanks
thread with perennial invention (rose vespers).

4.12.21

38

My providence is the beginning & the end
of a hopeful state of mind. An *Ocean State*
so grounded in the deep floor of reality,
where every man & woman might be free.
For I am involved in mankind. Therefore, send
not to know for whom the bell tolls. (Eight

bells... nine.) The innumerate One, who begins
& ends. The whole scale, the entire octave.
Who plays the keys (all 88). The Minotaur –
strong beast, weak man; the hero, for an hour;
& the weaver of the fleece. Brave Argive...
prudent, patient, passionate (the one who spins

the wheel). So providence entails a loving
motive, as the original impulse of the spring
propels your dream. Like that *Octagon Mound...*
one labyrinth encircling 9 holes (deep-wound
wound). Soft-humming whisper-cave, carving
a smile in earth – icon of human-feathered wing.

4.14.21

39

Sunk like some archival clam, like Edgar Poe
in vaulted caves of his junk-jewelry capital
your chilly heart, your tongue-like soul
were tangled in despair – blind rut brought low.

You glimpsed her rood-door through the keyhole.

The rose is parabolic yearning, so.
Her limpid weeds will catalyze good will.
Your sullen prince returns by Newport sail.
Love's knot is octahedral oak (& diamond too).

4.15.21

40

We know how a heart smokes & smolders
like sullen fire under a mild spring rain.
How it will burst out suddenly against your will
in rasping char – exploding sparks. So still
before the storm. Thus words of the elders
warn : soft early meadows will not come again.

The kingdom of heaven is within you, murmurs
Nicholas of Cusa – peacemaker & hierophant
sailing home from Constantinople, as in a trance.
The perfect Paradise is simple sheepfold gate;
hence human fallibility is rectified (each instant)
by the charisma of that humble door (hers, yours).

So the ineffable soul shines like an April
bloodroot bloom – so tender & fragile, yet wild
(woodland-free). On the mind's Dionysian stage,
where a crippled heroine confronts the rage
of a labyrinthine beast (his tyrannical will
a microcosm of despair) – & saves our world.

4.16.21

41

I've circled back to my first neighborhood
in my old age. The families settled here
along the river, built their houses. It was
a foretaste of a form, an equilibrium, these
hulking flour mills... salt of the good-
life earth. Yet April turbulence draws near.

The world hangs on a crux of *Lex* & *Concord*.
Everywhere. *Since Lincoln's life cannot be had*
again, then for the rest, from my dread
sovereign's lips... Twin Cities Tomcat Sees God

Walk Through the Door of History's High Room.
Many's the apocalyptic end-time men will come –
don't listen to 'em. No one knows when
the *Sun of US* will shine, at last (neither Putin
nor Xi). & many's the minted, minimal Max Milton
will go blind like me... before that Day of Restoration.

4.18.21

42

In the beginning were the folds of a rose
too simple & too deep to be expressed.
This ordinary life, primordial.
Our lovingkind, to whom we bid farewell.
Dream-wellspring in the mirror, like a ruse
of *eros* (leading us to find the one we missed).

He's gone now, in his long canoe... ripe almond
of an ailing world. Companionable Walt.
How far the soul flies from pragmatic earth.
How far we travel to conceive its worth.
Frail Prodigal! The *farfalla* (light-winged salt)
your royal sign – rude iris-arc – mulberry bond!

A faint rose atmosphere suffuses all (the
pillbox hat, the shamrock vale of Jackie O).
A dawnlight, or a double wreath. A chaste
equality of time, eternity (movement & rest).
Valentine's Day... or Boethius, with his *Sophie*.
More, his integrity. Penelope, knotting her bow.

4.19.21

43

Wisdom cries out in the streets, so the proverb goes.
Blackwell, in his rebuttal of the chauvinist defense
summed up like this : in our form of government
the state stems from the people. By their consent
power is granted their sometime administrators;
only in jury trials is it withheld (by common sense).

Pious Aeneas carried his father on his back
out of the burning city. He too was a father
& a burning brand, in the Elysian fields
of children's memory. So the heart wields
emblems of our origins – spirits of Shadrach,
Mesach & Abednego crane round Louie's tenor.

& in the inward labyrinth of Rose
the sun shines at the center, on the brow
of her rusty child; his smile a kind of *imago*,
her incarnate sunlight – bending like the bow
for an invisible neutrino, shed by Paradise
from the floor of Lake Baikal, bright on the prow.

4.20.21

44

Henry, the State grows fat, always wants more.
& More always divides – out of his head,
out of his jovial witty bloody body. He dead
or alive. Like that milky Memphis nickel, cut for
spare change. Like rusty Penelope, cheap date
out of Ioway (dumb cowherd, tending her state

of states). Meanwhile the planetary innocence
keeps mute – like that king of tomfoolery,
rabbi of royal mockery. Against the raillery
she leans... unaccountable (extradosed) countess.

Irish Rose. The longest bridge, a combination
box girder (cable-stayed), spanning the wide
narrow Barrow. Framing the little room
at Arlington. *As I have seen them tread the loom
at Whitsuntide* (pastoral dream)... sole bride &
windy russet sorrel (kindling love's free creation).

4.21.21

45

Literature is hero worship, writ that hieratic,
autocratic, power-mongering Pound. Head
sculpted at the violent vortex (by its victim).
The shining glamour of the prince marks him
the limit case, between Utopia & the erratic
melancholy of the ordinary. Living & dead.

Tomorrow, & tomorrow... Shakespeare's birthday.
Nabokov, too (invitation to a twin beheading).
England & Rus – St. George slaying the dragon
lifts his orange lance up to the *Suffering One.*
Green, black. Do not go gentle into that... *hey
ey yo.* The pennants in reverse, boots... wedding

like a funeral, at Arlington. *Anathemata.*
The Once & Future King (the children's books).
Man is the *animale compagnevole.* Navalny,
Alexei, felt that... so Maximus, so More, so MLK –
the prisoners of conscience measure *Maat.* Ah...
you feel it, now. The cosmos is a child's toy box.

4.22.21

46

to Heidi Slyker

The simple music slows time, the music
of what happens. As in *Spiegel im Spiegel,*
a mirror's mirror. A tongue on sad metal,
a mother's tongue. Life deepens, grows sick.

Each word, a tomb. A valentine from prison.

In his late light romance, a Boston Bean
lost her flute for 9 years. *Nein* years.
Heid to a skylark, rubbed wrong by sly curb, O
trompette marine – sunk-low b-flat will float again.

4.23.21

47

I think he will take this island home in his pocket
and give it to his son for an apple.

In the *USA*, the state of Rhode Island serves
as unit of measure – approaching the absolute
minimum. One can fit an infinity of *Little Rhody*
inside the state of Texas, for example. Only
Hope, its motto – the theological virtue – swerves
into its realm of the immeasurable, as St. Neot

of Cornwall knew so well (wherever that realm
might actually be). *Poor naked wretches, wheresoe'er*
you are... O! I have ta'en too little care
of this! *Let go the superflux*! – friend William,
Roger... tell me... how large, how red, how warm
translates the human heart? *Beyond space, beyond time.*

Near touching the absolute maximum (surmiseth
perspicacious Cusanus). The tiniest push penny,
the silliest Yak Bob... the humblest pinch-bumpkin
in the *Heart of Oak Society...* each van der Weyden
round-faced lamb – when Shick Shack Day cometh
all shall be folded midst her greensleeved Rose, Henri.

4.24.21

48

The meaning of this word, *providence*, in truth
must be embodied by the living, in a life.
That grim year at Sandy Lake. The refugees,
supplied by the Agency – pork & flour rife
with poison. Many died. Williams felt such ruth –
so did magnanimous Enmegabowh. Hard freeze.

The immeasurable gap between spirit & flesh
is wrought, engraved in every anguished face.
Yet spirit smiles – whispers *corraggio* (O *Falcon
Ace*)... just so our life & acts of mercy mesh.

*Not price nor money could have purchased Rhode
Island; Rhode Island was purchased by love.*
A grain of sand folds back into its *Ocean State*
(affectionate, companionable *polis* of immaculate
cosmos). & so the rude isle becomes a road, or
measuring rod : Blackstone's oak, with crown above.

4.25.21

49

In three dimensions (four, counting time)
the engineer, the sculptor slowly strive
to float a counterweight, conceptual rhyme;

to ravel a safety net around the hive.
All praise to their materials intelligence!
Intuitive *integritas* leaps up – alive,

proportionate – a beautiful consonance.
Yet I'm so famished for simplicity
my candle is a star... her light's romance.

It comes from far... our visionary city.
In seven notes, in seven days, the octave,
with its nine whole numbers, grounds infinity.

Her love's not something you might have
to hold. It speeds like *primavera* breeze –
it gives & grows more than you can conceive;

its circling refulgent galaxy will seize
your providential seven humps of Rome
& translate their meek minutes to always.

4.26.21

50

The adolescent green sheathing the cottonwoods
& the willows, the unruffled river moving along
like a brown mirror. April slowly turning
toward May. The leafy lilacs, just beginning
to bud, soon to grow pendant, fragrant, strong.
Ferdinand & Miranda (yearning across the boards).

Our life's an evanescent pantomime. The Minotaur
circles the ring. His twin, the Toreador, must
master himself. Rose snowstorms saturate
the Roman atmosphere, the gladiator's fate –
Caliban's a slave (perhaps a man, but only just).
How meek these martyrs in the frescoes are!

In the New World, there's a Jubilee, for 50 years
of states. It might be 52 someday (a Federal
Triangle – *O Carib Isle*!). It might be the beginning
of an old redemption. Out of an *Ocean State* (sing
sea-shanties, choristers!) an angelus perpetual.
Her little tree (holm almond) shedding human tears.

4.27.21

51

Nicky Cusanus, on board ship, sailing home
from Byzantium, was struck by a vision
of metaphysical otherness. The infinity of God
somehow smiled upon him – like some odd
Zeus, or some stray Orthodox-*qua*-Boethian
incarnation summa. Nothing was ever the same.

In the beginning was the Word, & the Word
was unpronounceable, unpronoun-ed *YHWH*.
Multidimensional trickster Papa (was She?),
undermining Pharaoh's awe-inspiring herd

of pyramidical bricks (along with his own plan).
Meanwhile, the good life of each cosmopolitan
& unknown *Everyone* paralleled the ineffable
happiness of humble simpletons... unable
to tell their left hand from their right. *Amen*.
The Word was buried in Jerusalem (by Magdalen).

4.29.21

52

That you tasted a morsel of life's wholeness once
in a little madeleine, or a memory that faded
doesn't mean that life is insubstantial;
only that the evanescent moss-green mantle
of these new spring leaves – shining, enfiladed
by wide riverbanks – marks a momentary confluence.

That sunny day, hitchhiking through the Adirondacks
you stood on a bright rise (hungry, strange &
all alone) and stamped your foot, & shouted out
in wild & simple overflowing gratitude. *The Spirit*
melted into you, that day; down from her high land
beyond our honey land – immortal & most holy wax.

Love is the source of all high adoration.
Selfless devotion & humility proclaim a goodness
high & whole – beyond all vaunted excellence,
beyond the dominion of this world. In such sense
take Roger's *key*, *that openeth a box of keys* : for this
unquenchable zeal, this fortitude, is of the *Son of Man*.

5.1.21

53

The insidious geometry of a grasping beast
is the labyrinth where every human heart
must make itself *harder than diamond*. East
to West, North to South, it cannot break apart.

A box inside a box, you said (with emerald ribbon).

The *gestalt* of your recital. Like a unicorn
of *shibui*. Black, white. Junk-diamond G-clef
in ruffles of tissue... just for you, Ariadne.
So broken Prodigal heels back to your rose *nef*.

5.2.21

54

Two gray-haired neighbor ladies, on the sidewalk,
by the driveway, walking their dogs, talking
quietly, this morning. One's moving back
to her hometown, somewhere in North Dakota.
They're asking friendly questions. No shock
they haven't been through, known (time's caulking).

Civilization is a sum of simple efforts. &
an effort at simplicity. That young girl
out the window, reining in her grey great dane,
like some Botticelli Renaissance Man
or leashed *condottiero*... O. Let scrolls unfurl;
one skipping kid outdoes your splendor, Ferdinand.

The distant thunder of a freight train
over the bridge. The rusty seesaw creaking
of a swing-set, like a mournful chickadee.
My heart, heavy as a trailing Cherokee –
but it's myself. I broke the vows, seeking
some brooding rose (beneath your simple rain).

5.4.21

55

The farewell glance of sunset on the backyard gate
makes one an accomplice in the great goodbye.
A particle of transience... infinite multiplicity.
Boethius, encountering Lady Sergeant Philosophy
felt the *lacrimae rerum*, & the Stoic mandate –
utter loss, bereavement. Job's excruciating cry.

& what does the poet say to the young Delhi widow
whose husband, the doctor, writhes for breath
without oxygen? Is suddenly taken from her
forever? She is angry with cruel God. Confer
with the angels – pray to the *One* beyond death –
Fire Spirit, before whom we melt away like snow.

With motion & rest, with chance & Providence,
with multiplicity & union... Boethius wove a knot.
So Lear & Cordelia join hands with their playwright;
so truth, compassionate dream enact coincidence.

5.4.21

56

The 5th day of the fifth-month, like lilac
quintessence of a Jubilee. *I married Isis
on the 5th of May*, sang the Iron Range bard
with rusty voice. Osiris sinks to one hard
scruffy penny, yet she'll weave him back
to Ithaka, Penelope – axle of the house she is.

Napoleon grew ever smaller on St. Helena (until
today). His little iron equestrian statuette
sits on my window shelf, exiled to Minneapolis
from Cape Vincent (last voyage for Odysseus).
So each *Colossus of Rhodes* compacts to *Rhody Lil*
– each *Faerie Queen* molts to kenotic kismet.

St. Helena found the True Cross for her son,
the shining Constantine. Byzantium came to an end
on Wednesday, at the end of May. Seraphic icons
shed benevolent light from Hagia Sophia... humans
travail more humble paths. Rude shoulders bend,
bear *angels, archangels... all the company of heaven.*

5.5.21

57

The old salt, eyes bleached by shimmering distances
washed ashore at San Francisco, years ago.
Looks up at me from his ship-in-a-bottle – grins.
Heard of lanthanum, kid? Atomic element, y'know.
Baked it into roads in China, once. They say it thins
particulates from air – clears smoggy circumstances.

Sometimes a sea-wind canters off the Bridge
& eases controversy into song. Like a lyre
shaped out of liars – like a topaz rain squall
slanting so seamlessly across the Bay, sea-wall.
Your hollow sound, sea-bell. Blending with choir
of tenders, tugs... sharks, dolphins... green sea-sedge.

I watched the sailboats criss-cross Newport harbor.
Remembered Kennedy, on board, lounging barefoot
by suntanned book; heard the soft boom shuttling
across your loom, Penelope. Crabbed scuttling
cannot erase the wounds, displace your livid root –
soft heartbeat, sea-rose. Home's trellised arbor.

5.7.21

58

Eternity, O Eternity! That is our business.

The immense crabapple a-flower over the garage
has reached her apotheosis. Like Japanese flute-
dancer (limbs akimbo, statuesque, hardly scenting
the air) she reaches toward some ineffable something
(apples? bumblebees? blue sky). Your courage
makes me memorize Providence... (my worries, moot).

Roger the pilot, on the crest of that rose town.
Steps from his canoe, walking on evening air.
His paddle welded time, eternity – Odysseus-oar
J-stroking visible, invisible (human, divine).

Your salt scent, wafting all the way to Minneapolis.
Rose trouble & betrayal, all my willful dust
of human foolishness. Time ravels to a knot.
Your soul achieves its apogee, Iscariot –
locked heart. We'll go to Galilee, because we must.
He speaks, the knot loosens... (Cordelia's strict thesis).

5.10.21

59

Sophie races around the house, clocked by her Mom
on Minnesota Statehood Day – her mother's birthday
too. Though born in Providence, Rhode Island,
she's now residing in her name-day state – &
is her father's counterpart (born on the Statehood Day
of *Little Rhody* – in 1952, in Minneapolis). *Welcome.*

What cheer, Netop? *The government shall be
upon his shoulder.* Emperor Constantine founded
Constantinople on this date, in Byzantium –
authority there authorized by that mysterium
of eloquent sweet light, oozing down from Hagia
Sophie. *Yet your* theosis *is more deeply grounded,*

whispers seraphic simple Maximus. On a black
prow, on a cinder-ship... on a Wednesday
(at trumpet's rooster-crow). Like a Lincoln penny,
smudged, meek... like her kenotic ceremony
on Good Friday. The *king of kings* is coming back –
in form of dove, Jonah. *Coo-coulombe.* Hallelujay.

5.11.21

60

Valentine, in his osier cage, the gentle father,
woodpecked his letters on pink dogwood blooms.
They all spelled *HOPE* – like Coke's long bother
for the liberties of everybody (Roger's air).

Our funereal labyrinth is like the catacombs.

Paradise was paralyzed (Penelope's tether;
Clover's veil). Henry was hopeless (his care
filled disenchanted volumes, huffy dooms). Yet
love abides – gold willow branch from *Charlie's Bear*.

5.12.21

61

My meek father John passed away this day
six years ago. He pointed up at the ceiling,
silently, & slowly drew a circle. & I felt
the glow of unseen far galaxies (heart's melt).
& I recall, on moving to Rhode Island, finding
traces of his family... Thomas, & ancient Jeremy

who sailed back to Hemel Hempstead at the end
to lie in the churchyard, under John Gould's Oak.
This was in Williams' time, & William Blackstone –
who nurtured the first apple in the New World
(his "yellow sweeting"). Those philosophical folk
(& public-minded) grounded common good in a zone

of metaphysical wisdom. An anthropology
of civil sovereignty – fostered in the shadow
of the *Son of Man* (the *imago* of Absolute
Benevolence). One deep-rooted oaken thought,
the apple of their eye : *Love is all ye need to know.*
Love is substantial liveliness (oak-gall cosmology).

5.13.21

62

Pinched lips falter on the lip of the flute.
Parched lips, not like these tulips (everlasting
for a day). Edgar Poe staggers down Benefit
past the Athenaeum – his yearning (passionate,
Hellenic) intertwined with his mad wedding suit;
his seedy self already bolting... squandering.

His dream, to inaugurate a *Journal of the Arts*;
with Whitman his helpmate & collaborator, they
would instigate a renovation, or a restoration...
after they were married. O drunken, fustian
thespian! Vainglory shudders in threadbare display!
Fever grapples with the flesh – the soul departs.

*

The *Argo* skims across lifeless blue depths.
Orpheus recalls their setting-forth, the grandeur
of the launch into sunrise horizons of pure liberty.

My Providence is something like *Aea*, in Colchis.
A sigh of vowels, or a breath of life; mirage
or Rhodian bronze image. Penelope wove this –
preserving Ariadne's kiss (gold swallow-cage).

Her sullen flame, unreconciled... immediate Medea.
Orpheus looks back in vain. Eurydice
has turned to smoke. The poet flinches final steps.

*

What if the Fleece is the Word itself? & the *Argo*

your homely canoe – twin rims of an almond
planted in Rhode Island? Its canvas a spidery
warp for ocean salt... its pilot, Ariadne?
Out of some cryptic labyrinth from long ago
a surfacing smile – tingling sea-bell *(Sauveur du Monde)*.

It was never going to be Poe's dream – or yours,
or mine. Like a cube of simple salt; like the sea;
like a gull's cry, her twin rowing wings of memory
Love surges with the prow, impels the oars.
Each halting effort homing back toward Providence
excels the keel, hums every spar – integral buoyancy.

5.14.21

63

I know next to nothing. But I know how lamplight
extends into gathering dusk, & how a moth
flickers around that steadier flame. & so
I apprehend all things are one (I know
this much). & if I can rise from my own sloth
my mind might comprehend : it's love, not fright

that binds this fluted seashell of phenomena,
this glittering Shaker crossweaving of stars.
& so we struggle with ourselves. These scars
are testimony – Lincoln's somber, corrugated face
a copper mite, a fraction of the human race;
Penelope keeps threading guile & hope (O *Shekinah*).

In a wooden forest-green farmhouse in Providence
(the Summit neighborhood, *132*) a weaver
booms her echoing frame. Or once did,
in my memory. When Alexander was a kid
& Phoebe, just a baby. So each Eve's a cleaver,
every Adam a deceiver – all awaiting soul deliverance.

5.16.21

64

Apollonius Rhodios picked up stakes & left
after a bad reading at the library, in Alexandria.
Failed poet, disgraced – holed up in Rhodes.
Kept on tinkering with epics, odes;
learnt lore of shipcraft, seamanship. *Aea*
was the aim... gold wool for his ineffable *nef.*

Ye shall all be salted with fire, keened Orpheus
behind the pilot wheel. Mirrors were mirages
on the edge of the scriptorium – all that fuss
of roundabout Odysseus. *We are but images*.

& *Medea*... rhymes with *Medusa*. Only the mirror
can save you now, Narcissus-hero. Ophelia
butterflies, chaste book... bears witless witness.
Pride burns sulfur-yellow (dandelion, watercress).
Edgar Poe straggles from Athenaeum to the bar.
Poetry singes the lips – Ezekiel-wheels (fiery Elijah).

5.17.21

65

In the mythical theater of the world, *Plutus*
(god of riches) almost rhymes with *Pluto*
(god of death). As *Mammon* almost rhymes
with *Money*. So those clinical, demonic crimes
against humanity bind their banality with us.
Your funds, George dear... watch how they go...

& the prophet is not without honor
if she has no country. The world arranges its
revolutions to accommodate power – but you...
it shall not be so with thee. The ewe knows
her lambs; the lambs know their green shore.
Love is transparent. Hatred ties itself in knots.

You seek the providence of Providence, Henry;
you seek the Seeker on the hill – soul unity.
Stubborn integrity. Yet it's from multiplicity
the feelings rise... involuntary memory;
the spare limbs of the trees, in that green park
of unfledged dreams. Forgotten helpers (Mark, Marie).

5.18.21

66

Slowly, slowly, George lost all the money.
The Bermuda Project vanished. Nevertheless
he felt serene, seated in the very cave-mouth
of Paradise – near home. LaFarge (Henry

too, later) limned a sun-gold lamb amid bare rocks

plein-air, there. It was an absolute quadrivium,
enfolding the impersonal with infinite *Paisan*. It was
the *Argo*, anchored in the Bosporus... *Argus
Panopt*, Hagia Sophia. Ruddy rood. *E pluribus unum.*

5.18.21

67

The crabapple flowers are already gone, & the lilacs
hang their purple heads, begin to shrivel away.
We climbed with Sophie to the Tower on the hill,
the *Witch's Hat* – overlooking her old primary school
& her great-grandmother's (Sydney Pratt).
The children were shouting, playing in the street
below. Pressed for accelerating time, I can't relax;
my soul is thirsting for some *Restoration Day*
framed like a wooden teardrop (water shaped by axe).

Nature this season spirals toward teeming *plenum*.
History trudges haltingly behind, a military parade
or ceremonial procession that gets lost, somehow
in yon fetid bug-infested swamp. Napoleon now
no more sleeps in exile on St. Helena. St. Helena
& Constantine were fêted on their name-day
yesterday. The crash of sacrosanct Byzantium
will be remembered for another year, decade,
aeon... (while Orthodoxy waits on her *Millennium*).

A sullen flame flickers behind my retina.
May be the smithy of Prometheus, the shipmaster.
May be the forge of Jason – hero of forgery
brazening out his exponential Pontic thievery
aided by Orpheus & Hercules... Medea, Ariadne.
Somehow our Golden Fleece is woven with disaster.

In Providence this son of *J* crossed paths with her
(portentous weaver of a cloistered tapestry).
The hollow oak that shades her mystery
nurtures an *apple-gall* (its wasp, its woodpecker).

The same flame burns in the North Star, the axle-
tree. The light for Jonah, in his submarine whale-
boat... the lamp for *Columbia*, of *Liberty* (lifted over
the Bay). O *summa*-dream of poet, lunatic, lover –
bright-glimmering brazier-glance of St. Kues, the gleeful!
When mind's most troubled, fearful... heart is hale.

Napoleon is in the grave, & JFK, & Camelot
is but a chimera, only a memory. Heroic grandeur
cloaks the guilty predator – the vulnerable Narcissus
(infant plant). The witnesses of historical process
are buried in the mud of mass extinction... each
injustice, every lie paid out (on desolate beach
& shattered arbor, wounded field). & for what?
Books, rocks? Lips tremble. Conscience will endure.

These lilacs, drooping... one man's time grows old.
Oblivion rocks my sleep, like Atlantic waves.
Unity & multiplicity... vastness, intensity... Yeats
chanting in his lonesome witch's hat (loves, hates).
He wrote for the Providence papers, once –
a tourist guide to Ireland's emerald legends.
My own *Noh* dancer, my Medea, knits her fold –
tragic betrayal, a woman's lot. Her face engraves
my Lincoln penny – island rood (her humble gold).

5.22.21

68

The abstract of the race was only in the mind of God
as her eye swept like a sea-wind, soft & moist
across the limitless ocean of the universe.
& when she whispered, *Partake, little cosmic face*
& you realized she was addressing *you* (wee lad,
lass) – you felt a newborn personhood, & you rejoiced.

Likewise, in some lowly way, the project of the cosmos
was a project of that *Ocean State* – that Providence
you carry around, like a turtle hefts her home;
a portable Paradise (*only a promise*, per OM).
Portable & changeable, according to circumstance.
Local, intractable – stubborn sailor's knot (or *SOS*).

The wild rose alongside a Little Compton shore road
recalls nothing of the bloody history. Yet the red
tinge, & the plangent scent, & the sharp thorns
serve for *stigmata* (Kennedy's, Lincoln's, Martin's)
& the simplicity of that sea-bell is for the dead.
Each face bears witness – every blessed salty node.

5.24.21

69

That frail dark steadfast pine across the street
framed by stretched limbs of two ash trees
against the sunny blue of a late May noon.
What kind of whisper can contain you (Alisoun,
Martin... Osip)? Hold my windblown memories?
Two lips keel over, peel upstream... arose complete.

My father & mother in adjacent urns, hidden now
under the soil at St. Stephen's. One silver cup
lifted aloft... strange hovercraft, stone prow
of grail. Ivory casque a gentle Elephant gave up.

Those Viking almond-seeds, sailing, rowing ahead
toward azure Byzantium, Black Sea – *mandorlae*
of transfiguration, crossing Whitsuntides.
The human heartwood all time's ebbflow rides
emerges like monarch from worm : the martyr's *ah*
an infant's cry, May morning crown (Rhode Island red).

5.26.21

70

i.m. Jack Whitten

That quick little woodpecker leaps up the branch
in quantum hops, hunting grub for kids –
part of the total totem, part of the alpha oak
itself. I inch myself along (toward obsolete-bloke
3 score & ten). In midway of Rift Valley trench
knock-knocks track thunder across Tulsa coffin lids.

& lost in fibrous tentacles of teeming clay
I'm playing jacks with Jack the chessmaster,
heartpastor – piecing his mosaic Sabbath day

(memorial). Eternal feast of the Recaster,
intergalactic steamboat shell (of shining whey).
Stream-tesserae of equalities – O Spirit-Taster!

*

The Mind, Henry, is neither Dynamo nor Muse.
Chaste measure of our own deluded globe, writ
Nikolai, & he was right; it is Ophelia's tears
beneath her veil of clover – her in-woven heart.

It is the Two-in-One, sans separation or confusion

as Maximus once whispered, with a feather pen
between his teeth (in his far prison cell).
Tracing patterns of St. Valentine (green acorn
heart). Shadows are light. *All shall be well.*

*

The shadows of men bent over, beneath the lash
of a self-centered eyelash – molded to its pride.
Never to escape the blood-soaked political hash

of famished idiots – nowhere on earth to hide.
Don't climb to the cliff-face, do anything rash.
Your profile emerges anyway (kings already died).

The mind is the measurer, muttered Nikolai.
The chaste mind, voluble vessel of love.
The light foundation stone, afloat in the sky.
Ground of union (equality, the treasure-trove).
The measure of justice & mercy is Providence –
her congregated candle-tree's unfading luminescence.

5.27.21

71

At a certain age, to approach a birthday is to recall
your grave. This wheel of earth, at the end of May
encompasses a little box – a grail, encrusted with
gemstones, threaded by fold on fold of linen myth.
William Blackstone, scholarly hermit, died on this day
in Cumberland. His farm, library... fire consumed it all.

William befriended the parish poor. He preached
beneath his *Catholic Oak* (catholic as in *worldwide*,
as *universal*). Adopted the child of a widow – married
her, in his dotage, for charity. So his heart reached.

Memento mori. Memorial Day. I remember JFK
as I remember myself. I know my soul freedom,
Roger, my recovery, requires complete surrender –
the Maker's wrath is kindled by the outraged honor
of original innocence. O chaste creation... kingdom
of gamboling kids! Let me behold your *Restoration Day*.

5.28.21

72

Cradled in my mother's arms this day
hidden in the green oak forest of good life
after many years I still repeat my infant play.

*

Restore us, *Abba*, *Sea-Bee*, deceased Dad! Strife
lops away the simple Good itself – its wholeness.
Emerald acorn, tepee-boat... *Mandorla* (beyond belief).

*

Scrolled against a State House wall in Providence
the Charter granted civil sovereignty; your *Rose* still
undulates through salty time (amnesia, indifference).

*

Art squares life as it can. My rude paint-spill
reduces infinite continua to earthbound clay.
True joy, awe – born anew – *Roger that.* Good will.

5.29.21

73

Cool & cloudy at end of Fifth-month, contemplative.
Color of bran, *matière de Bretagne*... gray
waves of sleepy memory. Rhode Island shoreline.
Where Roger dreamed *refuge for troubled consciences*.
Wherever 2 or 3 are gathered... they are friends of mine.
The pith of each wistful taps, on Memorial Day –
the battle beneath each war : to love, to serve, to give.

*When I was a child, I spake like a child... but now
I have put away childish things.* Roger's immersions
plant the kiss of spiritual fire, soul's ever-newness –
now they might pioneer *ecclesia*, carve their canoe.

Old times have passed on... yet the light shadow
of the great cathedral still circuits her ineffable
penumbra. The simplest things are most profound;
the smiling face above the offered sustenance
welcomes each refugee. *The stranger is your friend.*
The colors of *Old Glory* fade to greater glory : Abel
loving Cain. Human enmity undone. *Rise, walk*. Live.

5.30.21

74

May, the memorious elephant of months, curls
a mouse-tail around Memorial Day (recursively).
So each temporal finite shell ends in fine pearls.
Brescia Casket is such a one, clean tickling lips reply.

Cool ivory keys. I return to that Louisville photo
(summer, 1960). Suave smiling Uncle Jim, splayed
over a rocker. Grandma Ravlin, marble, sewing, so.
Dove-sister Martha. Sweet dark Juliet, who later died

too soon, too soon. One bass note (mute, *pedale*).
Gentle drone of iron. Time's heartbeat. *Adios, vale.*

Wind-sway of the Golden Gate is elegant, Byzantine.
Through its airy interstices small feet might fall.
I still see you, Juliet, when I reckon the scene
of painful adolescent grief – lost love's blank wall.

The happiness on that Louisville porch. So natural,
so tangible, so calm. I listen for a far-off Sabbath bell.
We might return to life somehow – simple, whole.
If only we turn the ivory key... walk back from hell.

5.31.21

75

June. The door to summer's woodland orioles.
The planetary summa. From the pine-green
bird's-eye view of Maxwell Mays, the capital's
a children's nest – First Baptist's compass-needle
gleams in the matrix of our peaceful scene.
John, the Seekers' founder, cries : *O Ship of Fools*!

He's eating locust beans & honey in the desert,
wrapped in lion's pelt. He baptizes with water
salted with fire, beside the Dead Sea – our hurt
he heals with truth. Our clay turns to the potter.

& as the time dives deep, & as the year's immersed
in the complexity of summer's *Ocean State*, we may
inquire – *what be the import of such fiery trumpeting*?
That other Maximus, in his Cherson prison, shall sing
more sweetly... lifting the almond rod of bright Mary
he'd trace the blue horizon line's incarnadine star-burst.

6.1.21

76

When your ship comes in, sister (*the Return the Flower
the Gift*) she won't be a battleship, but a bottleship –
her hull all dark wine-green translucent glass;
her cordage will be Noahide, & the merest fillip
of air will stretch her canvas by supernatural power
to the ends of the earth (a clipper-covenant of justice).

*I have received your messages of love –
as they leave your lips, they dissolve my skies*
he mutters, for the providential reader of the future.
In Providence (that bookshop by the Avon Theatre)
I found your letter in a bottle, Osip. *Paradise
a portable home...* (buoyant Pushkinian treasure-trove).

The smoke from a flame rose on the prophet's lips
& amid the snowy summits of clear apostolic air
a rainbow arcs above parched stones of Ararat.
The blue-green planet but a garnet pebble... skips
an ellipse across hovering lanterns in the harbor.
Chords of human & divine communion sound. *Fiat.*

6.6.21

77

Calm sky of pastel pinks & blues closes a burning day.
June swelters in a hazed cacophony of men.
Yet swathed beneath lost tamaracks, your *shibui*.
A showy lady's-slipper (mauve *mandorla*, Valentine).

9x9 glisten your Argo-eyes, O meek transhumanship

& so LaFarge becomes his lamb, Hideo his Mount Fuji
Juliet, Ophelia, Clover, breach from salty brine
to shine again – three shriven souls risen over me
from one linen box, one ivory casket (yours & mine).

6.6.21

78

i.m. Elena Shvarts

A child's simplex perception of the continuous
oneness of everything may be the beginning &
the end. Perhaps the hidden treasure of wisdom
is not the fruit of learned pedantry, but foolishness
in the Russian sense; say, Gumilev's effervescence
in the face of warlords' brutal perfidy – the hum
of hive's equality, the buzz of human dignity he heard.

My mother built a wooden bathtub boat, trimmed blue
& white, christened *Sophie.* I gave her to Elena Shvarts
in Providence – she nestled in her Petersburg window
until the apartment fire. Love indeed sustains the arts

but immortality is for the soul. Man dies; the sun
sets on the sea; false prophets & false Christs
make havoc with bewildered flocks; & still
the *Son of Man* is yet to come. Humanity endures.
I hear the Pythagorean hammering of Noah's children
shaping a new ark – delicate as *Sophie* in the windowsill;
winged like Thunderbird; stronger than stone immures.

6.7.21

79

Along the Nile, the Pharaoh was the radiance of *ma'at* –
doing justice, bringing order from chaos, as divine son
of Ra, the Sun. Isis nurtured overthrown Osiris. Thot
guided the hearts of men – to do justice by everyone.

A little Nile-boat, the royal bathtub cradle, rocked
among reeds. Like a traveling sepulcher, gleaming
with obscure gemstones. Like a *dhou* much-mocked,
transmuted now. An oval tear; an almond (dreaming).

*

The *Seeker*, standing in a stone canoe, looks out
upon an *Ocean State*. His palm, extended, frames
a ruddy roseate line – dividing sacred human spirit
from each sacralized authority. Pharaoh he tames.

Meanwhile, that moist mandorla, bobbing on the water,
sheds a shimmering tear. Mutters emerge... the *imago*
of Evening Adam rises from his emerald sepulcher.
A simple coracle has won the race, he cries. *Love, flow.*

6.8.21

80

Henry Woodpecker, old Rhode Island Red, rudely
raps at his acorn dugout. Mining for honey, or
bugs in the keel – like fire cuckoo wasp, maybe.

While over in plague-baked London, they've unpacked
the *Globe*, finally! *Midsum Knight's Dream*, perchance?
Or *Ham's St. Vitus Dance*... (pieces Ophelia lacked,

alas). Conscience is the helmsman of the soul,
O Jessie O. – its scarlet royal seal's impressed

*
*

on Hamlet's tab, to swing his death-ship west
again. *Lambkin was crown'd to make us whole.*

The theater of authority reaches up the Amazon,
back to the grave. An Empress buried in Trebizond
or Galla Placidia, under smiling stars... the Queen

of Sheba, too. Henry set his compass by good Will's
Good Will. It is a Restoration comedy (script still
unread) of equilibrium – gold Providential *coup de ville.*

6.9.21

81

My road in the *City of Lakes*, so quiet & green tonight.
Near the river, by the former Shriner Hospital
for Children (soon to be a new Brain Growth site
for the University). So the museum-mind might amble
calmly – like that young ephebe, pacing her dog, spry
as an auburn Irish wolfhound, to the Mississippi;
in step with a comfortable retirement of everything
(the day's newsprint, croissants for lunch, herb tea).
So *Lotos-Eaters* passed their wellness-time... amusing

themselves, taking long afternoon naps in Alexandria.
Wily Odysseus, hard-bitten Jason (son of Jonah) –
such veterans of war & sea-voyage despised *accedia*.
Engulfed by water you cannot drink, enveloped by air
you cannot breathe, a person suddenly about to die
draws life through a straw. *So you must fast & pray
if the same is not to happen to you*, the Rabbi pleads.
The globe's a plague ward now. When hair turns gray
amusements pall. Last testaments indict our deeds.

My bookshelf holds an ancient flock of origami cranes,
tiny white bird-shapes Andy Moul taught Alexander
how to fold, once (30 years ago, in Providence).
Little Alex was alert for them – ready to wander
in the "woody area", track their calls into the dense
undergrowth, amid thick mock-orange & snaking vines.

An old man's memories are like a Chinese box,
a Japanese claw-fan. An Edgar Poe contraption
meant to teach the lamb the lesson of the fox –
red hair, red lips, quick limbs & heart's deception.

Prince Henry was a handsome lad, with all the qualities
to make a charming king in Camelot. A winsome
cavalier, bold on the field & clever in the chase.
Yet all the sanctimonious force in that bright face
could never crack the seal of his heart's tomb :
a petrified self-love no mercy melts, no meekness frees.

The quiet of almost-midsummer evening. Old man
ensconced in secret in a serpentine gazebo (here,
on Cecil St.) – his spivened wavy cedar octagon.
With effervescent Nicholas of Cusa, he would steer
a bowling path between his own grievous mistakes
& that wide meadow of unknowable & limitless
divine benevolence... the sparks of glee
that quicken us, like fireflies in their velvet space
of slowly-oscillating constellations – O bright galaxy,

O sonorous *Ocean State*! If only Henry had seen it!
He thought he saw, but it was only thought;
he thought he felt – but it was only arrogance,
lust, vanity. A willfulness of insolence,
the acrid tar of young men's broken brakes.
While curious Alex crawled beneath snake-vines,
hunted through waste lots, rust of old cans...
Hearkening to early-morning fleeting melodies,
more alone than he knew – an orphan in the trees.

*

So the tiny rudder-shaped non-island at the corner
of New England sheds another flake of iron ore,
a fractal fraction of inconsequence. Smaller & smaller
this one shrinks, toward nonentity... the salt shore

opens her fan of soft wave-particles, breathing.

Jason's at sea, his mind still knotting Ariadne.
His flimsy heart turns to the ocean's cry.
Gulls flicker their wings against a sunset sky.
Dark motes. Waves rock the *Argo* (gently, gently).

                    *

We are Hagia Sophia with a million eyes,
muttered Osip, sketching like a Black Sea sail
his *nadezhda*-conception of transmartial Paradise.

A mote of salt in the prophet's eye marks transcendental
continua of companionship – the great congregation
gathered by the shore of Galilee (lock, stock & barrel

free & equal) for eternity. So salt is a sign,
like that meek-lowly tarnished-copper penny (etched
in suffering & glory) that pays out our redemption

once again. & I remember Penny Williams, fetched
from Providence to serve the dignity of veterans.
That dark Penelope also, whose lambswool stretched

across the loom of her own shattered heart – who owns
my own strange crooked one. *One grain of sand,*
one drop of water in the deep blue sea. It groans,

the Earth, with giving birth – these pangs we understand
because we feel them – in that little cube, that box
of universal salt we share. Equality we comprehend

with all the subtlety of Thierry, & all the orthodox

92

high passionate ardor of Maximus; with joy profound
of ever-brimming, spinning Nicholas – noting his tracks

both straight & curved around the rolling ground
of *Jessie-Jonah*, human dive-buoy – surfer in
                                Massachusetts
lifted from whale-mouth, like Moses... (by the sound).

*

William the shepherding wolfhound's birthday, today.
But something greater than great Yeats is here –
a spinning *Jenny*, raveling her woof so near, so dear
your heart is woven into Providence. *High Jubilay*!

*

Berkeley, the philosophical Reverend, was resting
in his favorite secluded spot, in a shady cleft of rock
beside the sea. Near Newport – *Paradise*. Nesting

like wayward Charlie in the royal oak (that square flock
of Roundhead materialists could never find him there
inside his acorn coracle). The mind is not to mock;

the mind is meek to understand. The vast bare
wastelands of dissolving history are prison cells –
are man-made deserts of malice, morose despair;

yet in each frozen corner of these rat-infested hells
you'll find a valentine from Politkovskaya, or Boethius;
you'll find a message in a bottle, humming spells

of human wholeness – hope. *Coraggio*. He's with us,

93

Emmanuel. Emma, she's with us, man. Never fear.
That free & universal refuge Roger promised once

is founded on the Scone of human dignity, my dear –
your birthright, like the birthmark of that rosy State.
The *Son of Man*, the *Daughter of the Sea*, draws near

today. Such is my Valentine's message, at any rate;
I fold it carefully, as Alex did, so it might float
along the breeze like some majestic crane. *Create –*

be born, be borne. Listen for that high *C*-note
the bass *trompette marine* thrums, questing, cresting;
skim across your wave, Jonah (O cool hum-boat).

6.13.21

PART TWO

82

Oblomov, indolent aristocrat, drowses in the shade
of his gazebo, flimsy cedar octagon. His dreams
flow into limpid summer – Olga's flashing eyes,
light laughter, serious brow... a grouse drums
in the cattails. Gawky heron lifts her blade.
We're in the middle of nowhere; Siberian skies
are cobalt blue. Oblomov misses her today.

A waning ember smolders in his heart – the last
link. The desiccated knot, shrunk to a diamond's
indestructibility. Brown penny, smudged with dust.
Immaculate center of the universe (crushed almond).

Olga, I might write you a love-note, if I may
mumbles the diffident shy nobody. The high stars
glide through their remote stations... pure silver
motes of silence. Their geometry is music now.
Man petrifies in avarice, grows deaf to choirs.
Complacencies are crystalloid. Redemption... how?
The rose blooms on your lips – was always there.

6.23.21

83

Yesterday, Midsummer Day, the solstice.
Jean Baptiste – his light begins to wane.
The planet plots her stately revolution
by those twins, those Galilean cousins –
lovingkindness & repentance coalesce
in perfect mercy & new life, children

they harmonize. This faded way of speaking
has grown shady for amnesiac America –
only holy fools & broken-minded freaking
Jesus-maniacs still dabble in such esoterica.

We're babbling in bartered tongues, shipmate.
A glossy glossolalia, metered by cash.
Mammon whisks away the commonweal
with cardboard sets, Potemkin sex appeal.
In Providence, Rahab rinses one salt eyelash.
Solidarity's the key to Jericho – opens the gate.

6.25.21

84

If *America is essentially the greatest poem*, then
Rhode Island, apparently, is the shortest stanza.
Shorter than Delaware. You can drive across it
in a half an hour, almost. Her *minimalia*
lurk in my Minnesoaty heart, her stubborn
quiddity – bent streets of Providence inhabit
me. Old wasps' nest... salt-muck shore for refugees.

The dream of civilization hovers like a prophecy
over sweet wobbly cribs of every stranded waif.
It is a plainsong liberty. Kings & their mystery
fade back to Shady Oak, make way for common life.

Justice is equal birthright of us all, grand Roger sees.
He lingers on his pedestal, atop the little cliff
over gray Providence. Steps raptly, blind, from
his canoe, into that Sunset Land... vast Western air.
His visionary ship of state is just a little skiff,
dubbed *Everymanwoman*. She skims toward home –
& in my microcosmic dream-ocean, she's almost there.

6.27.21

85

There were brawny folk who could drive the machines,
& plant the grain. There were whiplash money-men
who could captain them toward El Dorado – until
they didn't need them anymore. & so the dream

sank to these dried-up country towns, beseeching.

There were those others, underneath – roped in bad will
(with fear, foreboding). There were the sleek ones,
overhead – clinging to the contrails of the money-men
like herds of Bashan. *Lift us from the deep, Trireme.*

6.28.21

86

Every poet wants respect, like an American.
Your selfie steamboat wobbles puffily upstream.
But what's equal to what? We are the insubstantial
scaffolding of origami cranes... in a dream
you bent a little paper hat into trireme – let's call
her *Frisbee* – & set her off down Arthur Street, one
spring morning (1952?). To find your Guinevere

again. *Who do you love*? You're just an extra
something to read at intermission. You're a heart
on the cusp of a Valentine, or tears – not too smart,
my child. A rose in melting ice. Be quick, Susannah.

The eyes in the icon search the universe, right here.
The smile at the end of a game of ninepins (whatever
that is, Nick). Penny Williams in the greenhouse,
green-eyed, skin color of copper-chocolate mousse –
on the floor of a wishing well, beside the little river.
Moshassuck, *moose-trough*. Providence. Flows
in a trickle, out of Lincoln... rocks Venetian gondolas.

6.29.21

87

The primordial rose in a child's untroubled adoration,
like the infinitesimal point from which all magnitude
proceeds. As a soft insouciant showering rainfall
from a forgotten neighborhood fountain lifts the mood
into your infant primavera trance of time's *pleroma*
(fullness of equal counterparts in concord – union).

& beneath the unceasing patter-murmur of the water
the singular scraping sound of a one-stringed *gusle*.
Oars astringent testament of dissonance – Galilee,
suffused with local radiance of Rabbi Inventor.

& at the end of June, beneath a pendant evening sky
(*shibui* blue), Sophie will mime her Tokyo folktale
of the cranes, their silks. & *like Hagia Sophia
with a million eyes*, you hear the droplet-multitude
again, from an endless fountain... it will never fail.
Soon you'll be gliding back to Providence, crane-child.

6.30.21

88

In that summer time-before-time, a blue-green
upright piano rests against a wall. By the front door
(at 509 Arthur). Silence envelopes all its black-white
keys – it's like an empty machine shop (Mpls. Moline).
One whole note fills the whole measure (in 4/4
time). Our life is such an embryonic oval terabyte –
a dormant mandorla (dreaming potential rhapsody).

The 4th is round the corner – fireworks near at hand.
American people settle down to grill, under the shade
of municipal oak trees. Green evening light will fade.
We have no kings beneath their crowns, in this free land.

Always the ship leans upright, full of unplayed melody.
Unheard scales fold over scales... the sound
of Armistice, far-off parades. Peace was concord –
major & minor, sharps & flats... tensions resolved
in floating marvelous invention. Everyone's on board.
Invite them all. The pilots share their table round –
Marian, Jessie Ophelia, Jane... we too, beloved.

7.1.21

89

Blackstone preached beneath his "Catholic Oak"
in Cumberland, in the 1650s (*catholic*, as in
universal). On the run from English bishops
& Boston ministers alike, yet still he gospelled –
he was ordained. The law of which he spoke
being, the *law of love*. Normative – preordained.

Everything we say & do is but a summary
of what we saw before – incommensurable quiddity
of newness, like a dream. When God appeared
in fire to Moses, he was as unaccountable as we –
his gift to Man not rituals, but reciprocity;
so to fulfill the Law became lifesaving inquiry.

Roger, bright manic iconoclast (Blackstone's
unstoppable *camerado*) was steeped to the bones
in Edward Coke's good faith toward common law.
E pluribus unum. Equality of justice is union's
keynote – a plangent concord out of many ones.
& thus primordial integrity emerges (oakleaf awe).

7.2.21

90

You were the salt of the *Ocean State*, the fireflies
of young summer nights. The sparks on the grease
in the machine shops – & slathering the fat geese
at the State House (sprinkling our city parks with lies).

& when I walked down College Hill, in the seedy '70s
into actual Providence, free of that ivy enclave
I was met by Kennedy's VISTA volunteers –
I lost me, found myself (wingspread, eager to save).

Inventors of the common good... dreamers of *polis*.
Some gyroscope at the center of the heart
seeks integral union, its equable continuum – *whole
heart & mind & strength*. Love's art is all for this.

*It was not price nor money could have purchased
Rhode Island...* yea, the false prophets of Mammon
have no purchase here! Lips summon a communion-
cosmos, reconciled... *Eternity, O Eternity*! Compassed.

7.3.21

91

The tall oak, thirsty, sweeps its broomful of wind.
Fireworks rattle in the distance. Rough chaos,
self-dividing, rips down the highway. Everyone
is sullen now, Milton – night blooms have crowned
our independence from the king (his Hollowness,
his Shadowness). So in blind striving for dominion
every law forgets the face behind its bronze clockwork.

Creation is enfolded in the mind of God, as one –
who came to be among us as a servant, as a slave
& died one day (which is our solemn Jubilee). Wave,
flag of Abraham – your copper penny lifted up has won.

Rogue's Island was the last hold-out, the stubborn jerk –
thirteenth out of 13 (in a quarrel over paper money).
But she came round. Grandma Florence was born
this day, in 1900. Her brother died in the epidemic
when she was 17 – so she became an Episcopalian
(to break the impasse of despair). Phoebe & Sophie
flew to Providence today (the rose). Poe wrote *Eureka*.

7.4.21

92

I only show you the Rhody rood that was always there.
For Williams, the double-tabled Law forms a T-square.
Humanity intuits readily the 2nd face – it's 2nd nature;
the 1st is heaven-sent of God, for spiritual adventure.

In Nicholas of Cusa's game, you find God at the center.

America forms 2 great triangles, in Tocqueville's eye.
The center lies somewhere near Lake Itasca (probably).
The *Federal Triangle* was launched for civic liberty –
who christened that line? Virgo of Thierry, says I.

7.5.21

93

Henry, like Oblomov with the bloom off, suffers
declining summer light amid his octahedroid lean-to.
Your obscure henology, Hen! Your union-yearning.
Filters its glossolalia like some lonesome heresiarch
encrypted in cedar tesseract (from the beginning).
Yet he will rise again from his driftwood gazebo –
ineffable Ariadne, Ariel... the trireme's retinue hovers.

I see the anxious, lovesick face of Edgar Poe
loom from his Providence daguerrotype. The poet
nonpareil, compact, in Whitman's antithetical locket –
waxen offprint of disintegrating Time (its woe)...

These shadows in the mirror of a blue-gray lake.
Oblomov naps, succumbs to his memoir уютный.
Summer is infinite & deep. Man sleeps in her *theoria*.
Abstractions tack across puffed pinions. Noah's ark,
Argo of Prospero – your tugboat, Henry, of America –
Crane's Sargasso labyrinth. Nicholas of Clues, Thierry-
keels. A ludic masque (*Ariadne's Fleet*). Awake, awake!

7.6.21

94

The rain was pouring when we arrived at Chartres.
The brooding sky merged with the grey cliff-face
of Mary's house, high on its hill. I bought a t-shirt
(navy, with *Aigle* on my chest – just a local football ace).

We learned about Mary blue – her shade still gleaming
through light fibers overhead. That other Henry
here before (disconsolate anti-semite, dryly aiming
his lance between *Virgin* & *Dynamo*) missed Thierry,

somehow – who traced the trelliswork of providence
in seedy *formae naturae*... yoking the sabbath-rest
of the cosmos with a cloverleaf of free intelligence
(calm emerald ark, buoyant as delicate bird-nest).

& I remember that flock of ships in Newport Harbor,
large & small – *Black Ships*, battleships, yachts,
river rafts – bobbing like a floating arbor
held by Providential anchor – freed slaves' knots.

7.7.21

95

The Spirit moving on the face of the waters is beyond
our ken, murmurs Nicholas of Cusa (*absolute Maximum*
in his parlance). & the matrix of the microcosm –
stricken *Imago*, bronze *Koinonia* – magnifies an equal
                    bond
with YHWH, curling back to tie the knot (so in my end
is my *Beguine*). Mark this mobile endlessness, my friend!

Beyond our ken. Yet within the unfolding simultaneity
of the *Épiphane*, each step tiptoes in echoing concord.
Here's a treetop summer bird's-eye view of Providence,
by Maxwell Mays. One tiny steeple-mast (amid the dense-
green, supple canopy of civic panorama) sails toward
Ithaca, always… where agile, circuiting *Penny* spins
                    eternity

for me. Like Ariadne's catenary thread, drawn taut
out of the womb of Notre Dame – Thierry's lamp –
our mutual & latent longitude is seamless woof.
& like an acorn that becomes an oak (whose roof
is rooted in an *Argo* keel) benevolence has wrought
one Ark, one Jonah – walking on water (pilot-lamb).

                                        7.10.21

96

Self-evident means *equal to itself* (Ben Franklin's edit –
the skeptical, inventive businessman among those
visionary gentry-regents). Equality was *Providence*
for Thierry of Chartres – moving, material evidence
of that pellucid Dream from which it all proceeds.
The *Logos* : like some carpenter's trawler in Galilee,
skipping across rough waves with woody buoyancy.
But was the coin of the realm an Ecuador two-bit?
Ecclesia a smuggler's boat – shunned *Romany Rose*?

*Wherever the Judge's booty lies, there your heart will go
also*. For the heart's incomprehensibly intense –
dense as black hole (seething & smoldering).
So testaments of Sophocles & Shakespeare overflow
with Henry's morbid, guilty, conscience-shouldering
remorse – *the boy stood on the burning deck
of his own resinous, facetious dreck* (forsaken wreck).
At summer's orphan hearth... a child of silence.
Rain for scorned brow, *Pequod*. Heartbroken reason.

7.15.21

97

The poem wanders off like a camouflaged moose.
Near the line of the precipice, by the ancient
hunchback cedar. In the children's book, sprung loose
to rise again – after hunting season (rulers, relent).

You can't follow her. She's free as Beatrice, a bee
sailing a frisbee. All your imaginary yearning
is compacted in her hold (an acorn gone to sea).
Infant coracle, encircling its own equality – querning

nine rings (smooth ripples from a plummet-stone).
You see it flung like a comet, at great remove –
a burning dream. The ecstasy of plucky Madeleine,
enthralled with someone, something... *outre la douve*.

July. The fireworks are over. Your eye gets lost
in the infinity of summer... O serene Cézanne chaos
of equatorial green, veiling *l'Etat's* indomitable Dreyfus.
Shine, so, from your broken heart, *coulombe* (at last).

7.16.21

98

& of the evil that was done in those days... the tyranny
of fact without vision bears relentlessly down
with all the fatality of Original Sin. Bring your dream,
strange unaccountable child, to this modern scheme
of contrarian egalitarian humanity! Facetious life
summon, from your thundercloud of dark desire
(San Juan, beloved one). Calm *Liberty*, in the harbor
beckons with her torch beneath phosphorous Milky Way;
some basalt unison of wonder figures forth her crown.

The scapegoat King, penned in his swamp-oak hideaway
took all the hatred of the hungry crowd upon himself.
The inexplicable benevolence of fate was his insignia
(rose bee-stung seal). Curl up against the fray,
little Henry. Dream back to that milky magnolia,
Atlantean (your lover's arms). There you will meet
your equal, Wolf... her star-crossed waning is complete.
The orbit of her almond is elliptical; the continental shelf
lifts vast exactitude – to meet one smiling, circling pilot.

7.17.21

99

The rebellious pioneers in the New World wilderness
were there before Locke locked the gate on governance.
We Were There. The state of nature was no Paradise
for heroic yeomen – nor was the State a realtor's dance.

*Blessed are peacemakers; they shall be called children of
       God.*

Sunrise was a state of war. The Cherokee from Illinois
was passionate for Union – his lanky body was the glue
holding our delicate ark in one piece (*Ironsides*). *Ahoy,
Noah*! Your skeleton key's not land, but love (deep blue).

7.18.21

100

These damn'd tempestuous rebels in the colonies –
obstreperous sons of Cain, not Adam! *Livid the chasm*
branded across each Protestant brow! *Hot Scripture*
like a woodburnt stream tattooed on bones... pure
poetry perched like a raven on the spleen of Poe!
& that cathedral gargoyle, hunchback Benjamin Lay –
absolute John Baptist, *spewing hellfire every day*
on Quaker heads, in Philadelphia! O, *such qualities*
pled for Equality! *How steeply* Royal Oak *is off the beam*!

Oblomov, like an ox in his octagonal gazebo, grazes
against irenic Paradise – the perihelion of some
milkweed puffball, drifting into the blue. His Jesus
is vaguely orthodox, quiet, but there. Benignly gazes
through the shimmer of historical distance – the brush
just barely touching the canvas (Mont Sainte-Victoire).
Like Galla Placidia's tomb... she looks where *you* are.
The Shepherd, a feminine Sophia, will softly hum,
& his trireme will surface. Like a dolphin. Like a dream.

7.19.21

101

Jonah… just a minuscule Pip, spun from the *Pequod*
to the bottom of the sea. *I've seen evrathing…*
don' bother me. So small – smaller than Lil' Rhod.
Brown acorn become coral, become oracle – breaching,

preaching. *The law of nature being the law of God,*
writ the Boston scrivener, *there is no legal right*
for slavery in the State of Massachusetts. Odd
man out. *A person is a legal fiction,* this vast night

of silver fireflies – in the Milky Way, in the Ocean
State. Cézanne imbibed the symmetries of summer,
reveries of teeming nature, mountain atmosphere.
Dreyfus languished in his prison cell (American).

Individuals cannot be reduced to their classification,
read young Adams in his Aristotle. Who whispers
to me through this sultry haze, this petrifaction
of the facts? Pip… Jonah… grey-wingèd vespers.

7.21.21

102
for C.

A planet teems with multifarious self-regulating life
& a garden governed with care grows of itself
& the flourishing of happy kids is their empowerment
as they aspire to join the fun – so sparkling, ebullient
all around them, in the air. As equal temperament
tuned the blue-green piano, dear dark sister
so law's aplomb suffuses life with its pure intonation.
Unspoken, felt. Transposing mind toward some just
attunement – just beyond our jangled application.

Discord spurs the, sues for, rectitude. We want to play
as we always did, across the crumbling pastel keys...
me in the basement all day long, gluing together
my plastic *USS Constitution* – then hurling it away
in a royal fit, soon after. Your octave-spanning fingers,
long idled from those 88s by slippery malice (learnèd
bigotry). & that *your* birthday is the Constitution's, too!
Our pseudo-octave (*3/5ths*)... Union's *Judgment Day*
        retuned.

7.22.21

117

103

The hidden cricket whistles from the evening grass
enumerating summertime with tiny cheeps –
small self-effacing unfailing accountant, noting
the passing time, the fading summer light.
What your soul hath sown, so your soul reaps
in the immense Mahlerian oratorio (*Eddington's Eclipse*)
enfolding infinitely minor major harmonies, floating.

Equality is not the travesty of mediocrity proposed
by pure hieratic stylists of awesome Power. Nor just
the reciprocity of simple goodness (basic trust)
either. It is the Most High's immanent & perfect Rose.

The dove that floated from the heart of swallowed Jonah
(like a grey pumice gyroscope of grace) gave keel
& ballast to *the constitution of a rifled dream* – all
the cunning pursuit of legal eagles for that ultimate
serene Mont Sainte-Victoire of righteous commonweal.
Her *coo-coo* comes in little cricket-cries, that fall
across your sun-burnt paper heart, Maxine. *Selah.*

7.26.21

104

The tragicomic history of human absurdity reaches
way back, even unto Noah. Pilot of the Ark,
second father of the race, lying drunk & naked
in the shadow of his grape trellis. & poetry teaches
like a conversation – aleatory indeterminacy on a park
bench, suspense (your unpredictable friend, Shaked).

Thus equality must have something to do
with this awesome silence between I & Thou.
So the poem figures there – a pebble in your shoe.
Nutshell, apple-gall. A coracle. An acorn-*dhou*.

Unlike Paltrine, with haughty golden fleece, Shaked
considered not equality with God a spinnaker to puff.
Rather decked him out as common Galilee
sailor on shore leave (in St. Petersburg). Rough
sketch for *servant of the Lord*. Like you & me.
Kamen, akme... sea-vision of *communitas* (rose-red).

7.28.21

105

to Lyubov Sobol

That small stone bridge across the Arc, in Aix
at Trois-Sautets – "three little skips"– radiates
strange graceful elegance out of squat stolidity
(mundane engineering). Late watercolor sketch
for Cézanne – near the end of life. Postdates
those bathers, splashing through his paper revery...
a river-symmetry (twin arms, bending upstream).

Restoration entails not monarchy, necessarily.
It is a common rest day for humanity. Imagine
Lyubov Sobol in Moscow – standing up for Navalny
& the rule of law. Imagine the Rose of liberation.

You saw an origami *Mayflower,* in your dream
float down the Arc... acorn from Provençal oak.
Life shimmers with unconscious miracles of grace
beyond this world, beyond our simple schemes
of human recompense. This is one of the themes
of metaphysical poetry, my friend, my *Falcon-Ace* –
the wingèd freedom of your flight (each *Liberty*-spoke).

7.30.21

106

That woman waiting in line at the gates of the prison
with the others, holding a loaf of bread for her son...
she mutters the words like a febrile mourning dove
skittish with anguish – yet breathing her testimony still

while ships sail slowly down the Neva

From crown of your head to your feet shapes a vessel
as well (a human grail, suffusing omnipresent love).
So the Rose of buoyant balance lifts our communion.
Concord of unison with antiphon... from equality, *One*.

7.31.21

107

The paradoxical unreasonable reason of Creation
appealed to the quick translucent wit of Nicholas
(from Kues). & that flash of enlightenment he felt
on board his Byzantine carrack – powerful *Otherness*
pummeling down thunderstorm, athwart the ocean –
caused his frozen freight of human vanity to melt.
He understood no one can understand just right.

I think he would have loved such rough-hewn art
nursed forth by his coincidental opposite, Cézanne.
Humble, tired, indomitable objects slowly start
to shine, without budging – toward infinite vision.

Here, a smoky haze of wildfires dims toward night.
Crickets hypnotize themselves to the departing sun.
American enthusiasts prepare their party planks
& walk blindfolded off the ship of state, into a sea
of wrath. *What we don't know is what we shall be.*
Predatory leeches, card sharks carve their flanks.
Each human soul is God's own Imago (meek paragon).

7.31.21

108

When Jesus spoke of his *Father in heaven*, he was
also recalling his father on earth – all the kind fathers.
& when he spoke of his *Mother the Holy Spirit*
(a passage obscurely effaced from the canon), that
was in honor of his own wise mama, Miriam (who's
still the articulate mountain of sweet laughing waters).

August in Minnesota (the northern hemisphere, generally)
brings a change in the light, in the weather.
The boilerman sun leans back slightly, & you are
changed also – as with a dream (a phantom, actually).

The day is beautiful in my gazebo, muttered Oblomov.
*If only memory would serve me too – bring back
your smile, your warmth, Olga. Infinite grassland,
limpid forest, beckoning... that peacefulness I love
still resting, hidden in my heart. To understand –
to feed my wintry soul. Your hearth, a lake... (alack).*

8.1.21

109

In the morning, when fresh air holds the smoke at bay
& you hear the sound of waves, as they have come
& gone – each rolled like a hand curved round
with cursive blessings, from a point
near Hatteras Light... you will pursue that sound
through its grim porthole (dawn's black-white film)
on chickahawk wing, skrying shark-auguries of yesterday.

Through concentric circles of broken symmetry
the smear-slathered periscope, nausea-submerged
strokes toward love's hovership. Your longing, urged
like Lancelot's, like Jonah's lack... *rise from the sea*.

A black pip, a pebble... a flickering, skipping figurine.
Infinitesimal seed-grain, unmoving, marks the pivot
of pleroma, dolphin-child. All-hands' communitas
is singing there, aboard ship, crossing time's disjoint –
a convex valentine of equilibrium (*Nadezhda*-sighs).
Anchor for sky-trireme... O chartless Paris pilot!
From the center, Time renews itself. *Wave, Queen*.

8.2.21

110

Your numbers game, poet, your Pythagorean distinction.
Like the exactitude of the shipmaster, taking
the measure of the sea by its own buoyant means.
See-saw landlocked umbrellas are there none
where Ocean throws its force against your lines –
no demagogue will mouth your pithy judgement (binding).

Each strenuous talent brims with stringent discipline,
its limits strictly taken to their limit; just so
these *shibui* kabuki kids, flexing in Tokyo
outdo themselves alone, surpass their aim, when
besting every rival in the world's whirlpool...
Simone found equilibrium, balanced on her own steep
        rule.

Through Jackie's rose sunglasses (off an island
that is not an island) you might just make out
the *Round Table* of absent Camelot. An Irish dolphin
undulates like Weaver Rose, warping the waves... &
Roger stands, rooted – discerning pioneering pilot,
neatly threading between salty church & stately sand.

8.3.21

111

Henry, of that judicious, supercilious Adams clan
– after his 4-leaf clover folded (desiccated, veiled,
flattened in a tome) – beheld the morning Virgin
on her high hill... to which his Dynamo was nailed.

No man's an Ireland, boomed heart-heavy Donne.
For whom the bull toils, Hemingway droned back. Waiting
for his dense, immaterial anchor to hit ground (*my son*,
my son). The sea is bottomless. The ray will sting.

Thierry enfolded his conceptual *Virgo*, like one swift
clipper ship tacking upwind. Effortlessly the cutter
curves a turquoise paper wave. Unfold it... *lift*
us on your breeze, undying Life! Your love is utterly

beyond our ken, beyond compare – your valentine
a breathing rose island, enfolding Providence.
The globe's Olympiad – a game of spheres : nine
boomerangs (ineffability to ruddy immanence).

8.5.21

112

Dr. Harry Calypso, late of Hartford & Key West
was found comatose, at 12 midnight, badly battered,
lying in a gutter, across from Harry's Bar
by longtime colleague Professor Yu-Kee... are
you there, Professor? *Hemingway was a beast
but Harry started it – smiling, like nothing mattered...*

The head of Yale's Snowology Dept. shook his head.
*Hard to explain. Calypso popped his steel drum
between poetry & anti-poetry, between gnosis
& kenosis... Listen, have you seen Marsden Hartley's*
8 Bells' Folly? *Crane, trailing his daemon to his doom,
famished for one absolving* Word... *Hartley supplied.*

In code. The two halves of his *Bridge*, aching
like sun & moon – only to meet at (*figure 8*)
vanishing point. Salt tears of mournful sailors
melt each weak truncated *Hagia Sophia* – O luminous
compassionate light sent down through every breaking
heart! So the smile of Simone Weil signals, *checkmate.*

8.6.21

113

Meshed in the sultry dogma days of August
I cannot telegraph *what God hath wrought.*
All ones & zeros skitter in their dust.

Down in a forlorn storage cave, her notebooks
& bright paintings ripple through their solitude.
My mother's fingers coaxed these tender looks,

this Cézanne microcosmos... no, this Ravlin world.
The One is born anew in everyone. Such calm intent
makes Everyman the Son of Man (kind palm, unfurled).

8.7.21

114

Berryman, distraught, wobbled on the ledge
in bitter January – wedged between those faulty
sempiternal pillars (father, mother) & his own
Henry-guilt. I bide his maroon reflection, Bones.
Through the glass of my dark fish museum, Hartley
hooks his gnashing, weeping icon (hearts on edge).

His mourning echoed through collegiate hallways,
his caterwauling loud, awkward as Job... impious
impropriety! A crush of woe (disconsolate, unruly)
reflecting, in its backward mirror, crazy Jesus –
love is strong as death, jealousy cruel as the grave.
This trinity of love, grief, resurrection – won't behave.

Stevens was better, purer than us all. The voice
of a solitary soul, of you & I, must be well-girded
for *les requins & ouragans* in nature's melancholy
nightmare – *oui, mais non? C'est vrai? Mais la vie...*
C'est toujours bittersweet, Simone. Enfolding Mind
put fortitude by questing intellect – illness near grace.

8.8.21

115

My creaky cedar octagon leans & wavers in the heat
of sultry August evening. This cricket stillness is akin
to unity – your *one-one-one*, abstracted from the din,
identifies equality, subject to variation (Whitsuntide feat

of Einstein proof). Providence, for Thierry & Boethius
was like a sabbath of necessity – immeasurable snowflakes
of ineluctable chance (hummocked in remakes
of iceberg memory). Rose pebbles, unknown soldiers...

times you surfaced into jagged eddies, treading like Jonah
with a joist of recognition. *God is love*, muttered
the spark, the quark; when you kick yourself toward
her, she becomes your strength, your magnanimity (*ah,*

butterfly stroke). My gazebo in the orbiting dark
starts to float... drops talons, hovers above
deep-anchored clover emeralds. O mourning dove,
measure for me your fiery fingerprint (fading ink-mark).

8.10.21

116

i.m. Toshihide Maskawa

The texture of the text, when you reach down
like Weaver Rose, or like Penelope in Providence.
Along the ineffably fine-grained, furry sheep's yarn
held in taut parallels, along the warp. Your sense
of touch at subatomic level (where quarks are born
& die). Snow falling on Mt. Fuji – on Nagoya-town.

Emerging from a tub, you might experience a Joycean
epiphany – watch twinkling hexagons appear, vanish
transposing oscillation with insouciant sketch.
You are the beehive, where from common vetch
gold honey flows into hexagonal & cosmic wishing
wells – yours the kind forehead, for whom galaxies began.

That invisible, hearth-warm vehemence from within
pressing back toward violence without... it's just
the just tuning of the just, enacting equilibria
of perfect imperfection; the restoration of trust
from dissonance, asymmetry. Then (within quantum
meadows of unprediction) a door opens : *Love = Person.*

8.11.21

117

Those heavy objects glimpsed in dreams – they may be
lighter than you think. That rubble of thick blackbirds
feeding through radiant lime-green morning of backyard
even if commingled 700 yottameters from your bed
by horsehair's flickering, slippery eels' refinery
will take wing any moment, instantaneously. Your words,
Wormsworth, are stonier than memory. A dream's
            discard.

August prefers to trundle by imperial chariot, bent down
with Jovian gold ingots. The prince is burning bridges
again. Senators are dithering. Our kindly barbarian
host offers conceptual apples; Boethius remains
            courageous.

We are going, and where we are going, is where.
These blackbirds are my family too, croons Galla Placidia
from the starlight of her empty mausoleum. Deep gaze
from the face on this shady penny... gone, not dead.
Not even gone. *Your voice which kindles my desire*
flows into my voice too – is mine, low coo-coo Joan. Ah,
now I see. Like beasts, birds, grass. Yet sheep will graze.

8.13.21

118

August drought in the northland (part of the general
apocalypse) reveals archaic rocks along the lakeshore.
Dark slate-gray, with furrows etched by Cézanne, Jasper
Johns – one, an elongate *Croix de Lorraine* (orthogonal).

My brother labors at a rustic monument, piles stones
above our parents' ashes – on a pine-swept cliffside,
facing east. Beneath life's arcing jet, a salty tide
(moonlit, fathomless). *Most High, hear our groans.*

The showy lady's slippers of the swamp are gone.
Only their dark-green waves remain. *MRG*
would have traced them, one way or another
(for the kids). The clay is full of martyrs, unknown

saints. Hum that old tune for me again, Isis,
Osiris... the one about the funeral barge of life.
Flowers are the glory of the wilderness. Strife
marks your birth-pangs, Jeanne – our crux just this.

8.27.21

119

To think of a Narragansett osprey's glancing view :
a child, shaping sand castles by the oscillating shore
while the summer sun (beyond a scrub-oak ridge)
begins to bleed into the evening sky. The falcon knows
the child's blood royal, too – the whole green floor
below is her domain; & yet she preens no knowledge
or concern. The royal *We* are molding something new.

The glistening sea at dusk turns deeper violet. Soon
beneath midnight black, transmutes to whispers (sighs
& groans). Berkeley's immaterial dream (wise loon,
stranded nearby). Westward the *Royal Oak* heels... dies.

We drift into the cold Euxine, eventually – into the total
Black Sea our *Argo* sails. Beneath hollow vaulting
of forlorn shoreline cathedrals, grey wings dip & skim
like aerial dolphins. Where Galla Placidia comes & goes...
Tiny grains of sand are slippery. These eyes grow dim.
But not those eyes, Jonah. *Liberty* herself is molting –
taking wing. Old Earth's *akme* of vision is choral (coral).

8.29.21

120

Your message from the past was like a limpid oracle.
An origami crane, fit to unfold within a wine bottle.
All dignity of human life was cradled in that coracle –
the sabbath of what happens. Rest thee, little mottle,

buoyant mote, embattled *bateau-mot*. Still, calm. Float.

The storms will rage, each passionate debacle.
Sullen treason, arrogant pretense assault your Triangle.
& that doubloon nailed to the mast, a shiny obstacle...
only the shadow of your candor, Penny (river-ingle).

8.30.21

121

That you are far-off there, Olga, & I remain
planted alone in this wobbly gazebo – while summer fades,
August declines – these are but accidental differences
of place & time. In substance we are one, being
in love (which is a substance beyond substance, One
beyond oneness). I am, as you see, still reading Boethius.
The sky's more blue through spavined planks, the clouds

more tender & remote, birdsong more vibrant, plaintive
through these prison-window bars. Happenstance,
        merely.
Clear air is more hieratic than Justinian's pendentive.
A simple quiet Sabbath day brims oneness, everlastingly.

Perhaps St. Valentine sent little paper hearts, like yours
& mine. Perhaps our accidental sufferings are pain
like his. Rude obstacles to love – & yet an opportunity
for us to flower, somehow; even if only in something
flimsy as construction paper – frail, fictional & fluttery
as origami cranes. *Everything that rises must converge*,
        Olga.
What strained with melancholy radiance... will smile again.

                    8.31.21

122

Williams, crisscrossing the squally azure of the Bay
from island to island, paddling hard in his light canoe
or bending sail, following the wind, recalled sometimes
the *wilderness of the sea* – a cloud-shrouded mirror

of infinite oak forest, stretching trackless away
into the west. Somehow he kept a cheerful *corraggio*
& his barbed, intense fervor for righteousness, no matter
what exacting chores life brought... *O birthday chimes*!

For he was giving birth to a kind of tangled freedom,
a tiny new kingdom – anchored by hope, ballasted
by tolerance, good fellowship (each on board aware
they shared an equal danger, braving the storm).

*Not price nor money could have purchased Rhode Island;
Rhode Island was purchased by love.* Dry & spare
his message in a bottle, flung from *Ocean State* into
the spume... a *Jonah*-scrolled honeycomb, circling home.

9.1.21

123

Drifting off to sleep to the sound of *Capella Romana*
on my couch, one quiet rainy Friday in September
showers of rainwater mingle with Marmara shores
of glistening grey marble. Lightwaves echo & extend
their haunted, hesitant apostolic voices – climbing higher
slowly, by half-step, by quavering semi-tone –
      ALLELUIAH
they drone, below – an exaltation from the ocean floor.

In sleep polarities change places, merge together –
angelic-human, infinite-finite, woman-man... dream
& reality. The romance of a bearded Lord Creator
dispossessed by hateful envy, coming to redeem

his universe again, through suffering & love... it was
a way of muttering beside the fire – of rocking
between wobbling irreconcilables, implicate pairs
of entangled opposites. Red & blue in Constantinople,
black & white in Minneapolis. A single sail, tacking
across a lake... a sea-bell seashell, flickering whispers.
Inching, halting, glory to glory (toward humble Paradise).

9.3.21

124

In August the earth begins to tilt toward autumn.
A slightly washed-out sun rhymes with the gold
of dry cornstalks, the wide fans of goldenrod
shading roadsides, fields. I tagged along today
with Sally & Sophie – zigzagging through Dinkytown
to visit wrinkled, rustic bungalows of the very old
& frail (with *Meals on Wheels*). & it was good

to leave behind my own dry bookshelves for the scent
of random & impoverished chance, or providence –
the clean hardship of each empty-handed ancient
immigrant. She said she'd be making borscht today;
I'm from Ukraine, she laughed, *92 years old* – & bent
down, smiling, to thank Sophie (8). So the immense
planetary arc leans up toward unison (earthbound icons).

*

All my anxious learning is like pollen-dust of goldenrod.
Faith surges through enfeebled fibers of the heart.
& yet the urging *Logos* in the mind would heft its load –
lift mortuary spacetime like a mourning-dove Mozart.

9.7.21

125

Blinded by the dark maroon persuasions
of his own slippery tongue – the submarine
king of a clamshelled skull's domain –
he sought that pure *Eureka* no one shuns :

one silvery unmoving clear starpoint.
Amidst a perfect end-of-summer morning
in that dacha where once Oblomov, lingering
yet, yearned across the steppe of his own sunset

*

he felt hypnautical rose lips unfold a trim trireme.
The Black Sea thundered through its own darkness.
Earth gritted teeth, hauling its plummet harness.
A human cry went up : *Only to sail, & not to seem*!

Suddenly, vermilion cloudbanks anchored rainbows.
Showers slanted through sun's windward beam.
Your Ocean *berth was furnished long beforetime,*
Child, a murmur came. *My oaken keel knows where it*
          goes.

9.9.21

126

Summer was sighing slowly to a close. The leaves
were dappled things now, yellowed with transient
decay (the trees remain). We cycled downhill
with them, toward the convergence of the streams –
beneath the bluff, where the fort stands watchful,
a compendium of old buff sandstone bricks (the tent
of Little Crow not to be seen). The Mississippi sieves

through time & history – like a fifth element,
like a quintessence. Like that orthogonal direction
of Black Elk (heaven through earth). Like *Heligoland
with its one tree*, like Boethius with his quadrivium –
four ways, completed by a fifth (his execution).
Like his mercurial *Sophie...* whose Providence is twinned
with chance, whose grace unfolds each fatal testament.

Nicholas read him, & Thierry of Chartres – beneath
those arched gray granite limbs of human pride, &
prayer, & self-surrendering devotion. Replicas
of each soul's gravity (unto transfiguration – dream
of delicate intrepid monarchs, floating toward Paradise
or Mexico). Two bicycles, in tandem. Four earthbound
wheels. Ash whorled from towers, like an autumn wreath.

Boethius, Cusanus, Thierry... they sought the ground
beneath floating conceptions. Rational concord,
O Lady Philosophy. Substance of that ineffable source
of infinite fluttering multiplicity, the scheme of schemes –
the central omnipresent smiling *One* (beyond remorse,
beyond grief & despair). In the music-box of the *Word*
they found you – shimmering paramour, flute-sound,

trashumanar. The secret garden of the Kingdom.
Unfold your infinitesimal *Zhen Xian Bao*, the cryptic
peripatetic stone – & find the Person behind the mask,
beyond all figureheads & counterfeits. The hum of hums,
shkediya continuum – almond that speaks before you ask.
Rose road that glows, beyond the voids of intergalactic
happenstance. Sun-threads in the womb of soul freedom.

9.11.21

127

That lofty flock of black-white birds, so remotely high
in a crystalline blue. Gliding, turning in free-form
formations... Canadian geese? Aliens, angels?
High over the off-kilter wind vane, atop my rickety
Oblomov-hut – surfing jet streams past every storm.

The flickering, ephemeral light-brow of phenomena.
The mask of nobility, *personae* of a crane-bone flute.
This beautiful shimmer of coordinated flight, being
a fanfare of achieved wing-balance (aerial, buoyant).
Your ineffable heart & soul desire to sail again, *selah* –

to sail forever – singing, flying, trumpeting with joy
beside serene majestic wingèd ones like these.
Not to accept the 2nd-best, the consolation prize
of metaphysical epicures, pessimists – but seize
the promise of eternity... Eternity! (*O Happy Day*).

But as the planet spins unwavering into another autumn
& as this rusty Oblomov-mime stares into embers
of Nicholas of Cusa's *absolute minimum* – he dangles
like a scarecrow in a Bruegel panorama... his *kenosis*
tumbles in a clown free-fall. O infinite mysterium

of three blind men, toppled in one ditch! Yet
look again, look closer now. Into the microscopic
minuscule... into the rude Rhode Island honey-sting
of Providence, folded in a sea-rose (in a swamp-oak
vale). Your butterfly is weaving through the net.

9.12.21

128

My father with me in the basement, putting his hand
on my anxious, manic, broken-down brow. *Everything
will be all right, Hen*. Full fathom five, now. Enfolded
in his *Paradiso*, beyondsense – high above, now. Smile.
Oscar Cullmann, O. Mandelstam, sketch the same thing –
the Redemption has already happened. As a wounded
profile warmly glows, within its muddy copper band

out of all the different coins (copper, gold, bronze)
buried with equal honor in the earth (only bitten
by their age) – so the forthright flame of a human
soul outshines all counterfeit, forsworn doubloons.

& just as every king from time's beginning stands
as figurehead, or simulacra, for the benevolent
outpouring of one ceaseless, mossy waterfall of life
– a talisman, a token for that emerald Blessed Isle –
so the two faces of the coin (*Caesar* & *Christ*) are bent
across the gunnel of a reconfigured prow. Your wife,
Jason, Jonah. Ariadne's Pen (who knots all strands).

9.13.21

129

This deep sundown radiance in mid-September. Strong
breeze through the trees, limpid midwestern spaces.
Only the slightest motion moves tectonic plates
of buried memory. What you loved, what draws you
still. Perhaps a soft percussion invocation (traces
of one sultry Alabama summer). Sadness waits,
remembers. *Peace, child. Mornin' come before too long.*

America was just a trial run, rough sketch, improvisation.
Providence a mongrel colony – castaways, Narragansetts.
Its charter a patched-together, half-breed, homespun
contrarian quilt. *Sacred & civil...* (crosshatched tenets).

The red & the blue merge in the lowly violet (state
flower of the Ocean State). Nervous obsessions
of petty tribes shrivel the fan of summer sweetness
to the cash register of greed, the panicky crew
who dominate the kingdom by blind violence.
We're smart, they're dumb. Yet the rose scythe of
            Maximus
still drones his hybrid crown of gold, sapphire (incarnate).

9.15.21

130

Oblomov, rough transparent diamond,
sleeps in his September octagon (a rude
cedar gazebo). Olga traveling in Trebizond
will write him, in his dream. Life is an interlude

between main acts. Invisible *Father*, sparkling
Son... his coppery firecracker almond branch
snaking, like dragon on a fuse, toward *Kingdom
Come*. Your feathery pumice crown, wren Blanche...

I'm drowsy too, musing on *Restoration Day*.
Almandine threads Penelope weaves, unweaves.
Gleams in the sun. Her thimble, a copper penny;
fingertips tingle tiny cymbals. *Whoever believes*

in Me, they shall not perish... So lips keep the shape
of a paper ship, launched beneath pontific stars.
Oblomov's eyes are closed; a feather tickles the nape
of his neck. *Not Rome, but Man's place in the universe.*

9.18.21

131

The shadow of a goldfinch suddenly skims & dips
through these blowsy end-of-summer weeds.
Such leavetaking accents shape their utterance
as wrestling clay lips articulate a wedding pledge.
A ring, a bowl... their local unpretentious salience.
Out of treason, out of exile. Out of callous deeds
come to boil, burst, bust (prophecy's epileptic skips).

Emitted by nondescript gray pebble on the shore.
Refugee, veteran. Who harbors, as in sanctuary
copper tendrils of an agate whorl. A bronze door.
A stone's ellipses are their gate (*you'll see, you'll see*).

O goldfinch, wing me to your black-gold symmetry.
The jungle roars with human tigers – wounded paws
that tear each other for their shreds of dignity.
At the rim of vision, Earth's transparent edge
the hierarchies fade – angels assume the poverty
of flesh, kings travel incognito, unknown soldiers.
Law is clear as air : gold crown. A crossroad trinity.

9.19.21

132

Once upon a time, long long ago, in Providence
in a little forest-green farmhouse, down the block
from Miriam – the Summit neighborhood (*132 6th-
sense*) – a young family grew, full of good luck

& bad. *A Holy Song of Thanksgiving, by a Convalescent*

To the Deity, in the Lydian Mode, Beethoven wrote.
Slow, painful harmonica... sighs become eloquent
in resolution (*D.S. al fine*). The providential note
is gratitude. Beauty is truth – love, past argument.

9.20.21

133

The enormous limpid last-of-summer moon floats there
suspended over Earth, like the first apple of autumn.
Like that great sphere anchored over Narragansett Bay
we watched one surf-washed summer night, lifetimes ago.
How everything alive yearns to rise up, sail away...
levitate together in an airy wombship – *O mysterium*!
Rock-dove, *enfolded in the fire* – Reality we cannot bear!

Nicholas of Cusa smiles from within the labyrinth.
His *Game of Spheres*. The ineffable *One* we cannot know
is love's familiar otherness... close-fitting as a plinth
of warping copperheads in Cuzco fastness, gaunt Vallejo!

As if the laying-on of hands is like Lincoln's touchpiece.
We sense the billowing sail, the pliant mast, the keel
still faithful to its starry *Virgo*-course... a Triangle
of three ways at the crossroad, questing *Liberty-Argo*!
Yet the cargo in the hold holds firm; lights still dangle
from the harbor piers. Playful, immaculate repeal
of far-off bells! The perfect Love you zone is peace.

9.21.21

134

to Livio De Marchi & "Noah's Violin"

Livio De Marchi, of Venice, the artisan… who floated
a wooden boat like an origami hat, and a pumpkin,
& a woman's shoe… & now an equinoctial violin, large
& graceful as a gondola. *4 Seasons.* Let it be noted.

Praise to the simple men & women who can see
plain beauty in blue veins of marble, in the grain
of trees (*12 kinds of wood*) – & build a fluted barge
of hopefulness. Against that discord seeded by envy

& avarice – the insatiable void of greed for money
shattering the vines of *Union*, peaceful pergolas of Italy.
From *Giudecca* to *La Salute*… Mozart & Salieri –
rivals fused in a wedding band. Bright salt & honey.

The veins in the rock are formed by fire – the veins
in your embracing arms, for self-surrender. Jonah
through the grey vault shuttles, flickers into autumn light.
4 Seasons… waves of leaves. Noah's *Argo*, hovering nigh.

9.23.21

135

So you nestle, grey pebble, rock-dove, among the silicates,
in the ring or upper mantle of Earth's crust. Violet
mother-of-ruby, almandine. Simple mandorla,
catenary canoe... transmuted in the furnace
of the whole weight of brutal criminality. O Africa,
the woe that is laid upon your shoulders! Sly net
of thievery – ideologies of sleek deracinated syndicates.

The pebble nested incognito in the trireme's prow
is dual, bicolored, & veined with quartz.
Clear water of blood diamond – raying facets
like Rose Island Light (from the beginning unto now).

I would whisper it clearly, like antimatter photons
penetrating cosmic darkness. *Unity*, *equality*, *connection*
– a silver band from Alabama, set with almandine.
Rose lips (*Cabochon*-cut, in Connecticut) from
        Providence.
The legal *Union* of creation – manifold, playful
        benevolence.
Enfolded in a diamond *kamen-akme* (buoyant salience).
Chanting love's upright, crossroad law – clear as the sun.

                                    9.25.21

136

Evening arrives early in September.
The crickets are wheezing, drunk on autumn wine.
Their monitory note ratchets its minor wail...
an arc, an arch. An elegiac timbre (as if
by design). We will remember that full sail
after the first snowfall (O brief improvisation)
as we creep, on sixfold insect legs, across
the earth, lofting our windowpanes. *Wingèd one,*
inscribe your talons across our shoulders! *Lift us*

home. Oblomov-Noah, with his anxious dreams,
cannot luxuriate as was his wont. The dacha
suppurates with parasites. Clever, devious
termites feast on honeyed cedar of amnesia;
winter is bitter almonds then, beyond the pale.
Boethius, Maximus shared the same cell – it was
their doom. A spiderweb design, spun in Byzantium.
It was the entropy of gravity, that's all – the force
of spinning clay. Across onion fields, the seraphs hum.

*

Crickets lend their silver fiddle-voices to the choir
of the leave-taking sun. Everything remembers
its own end. The fifth act is Cordelia's; King Lear
follows her lead – to taste at last the ashen embers
of love's phoenix-flight. The audience is hushed.
Her sabbath-day gives pause. *The rest is silence.*
Lips are sealed. Fountains that once gushed
with glee are still pools now. Unreadable Providence

is *only a promis*e – the crypt an ineffable sigh

of long-suffering imprisoned air (at winter's end).
Chaste vision of Gumilev... Akhmatova's cry...
spark of the Covenant, whose dove-wings bend
searchlights of Coke & Williams into understanding.
Graceful *intelligence of love* lifts up the soul
into a wholeness past all *reason of state*, O King –
etched into Most High's *restoration* banderole.

*

Henry, Henry, to yourself it seems, sometimes
your elegant tongue-twisters only break your tongue.
& that model *Constitution*, over which you labored so
in a glue-scented basement, on Arthur St., so long ago
falls apart in your shaky fingers... which tried & tried
but not hard enough, it seems. Too many crimes
of white collars, callous clerks, perched on the top rung
of the money belt; too much complacent selfishness
mixed up with guile. I cannot match the vertical mast

to its horizontal beams. My Roger Williams dream
of *sacred & secular*, in complementary harmony
& free concord, is like a drafty old canoe –
its hoary, moldy bark awash with rancid, weedy
odors of that sloppy, flushed-out Narragansett tide.
Like they say on Federal Hill : *Whatcha gonna do?*
Nick of Cusa, Terry of Chartres... Boethius... *c'mon,*
Henry! Nobody knows whatcha talkin'... the scheme
ain't hangin' togetha. Just bein' honest whitcha, man.

& yet the trireme in your dream somehow remains.
Like that sacred & spectacular *Ship of Theseus*,
continuously maintained by replacement planks

153

still docked & floating through the Roman Empire
right in Athens harbor... Still the same boat?
Still the same ocean. Still tiny Rhode Island, sire;
still troubling the waters of thy *Charter*. Thanks,
Jeeves. So my Juneteenth Jubilee of 50 more possible
       years
remains in the cards? *It builds within – or breaks your*
      bones.

Soul liberty. The Lady from Paris in the harbor
shines her lamp through all that wilderness interior
of your own heart. Where little Providence lives on,
like the lone woman in the forest-green farmhouse
who wove the golden poet's poncho, in her hideout
on Wickenden St. (*Sheep's Clothing*). & the Unicorn
at the top of the stairs, in the house of Susan Brown...
she wove it, Sophie's Nonna – as a young seamstress
(in the distant past). Not far from Inverness.

I think of Roger Williams, striding down full of cheer
from the spiritual highlands of his charismatic gift –
an intuition that the commandment, *Love the Lord*
your God with your whole heart meant something very
      clear.
That wholeness is the bride of innocence. That the heart
of every man & woman is a child's heart, swift
& clean & full of free delight. & that such a gildhoard
cannot be belied, diluted or traduced by striving men.
No. Rather such love can never fade – will live again.

         *

So it seems I'm here to sense an aboriginal union
enfolded within our political *Union*. Not beyond,

not transcendent exactly... but different.
More simple, more normative, more universal, then.
Suffused, ineffable as photons, through a Narragansett
wigwam – the one where Williams, shivering exile gent,
curled up as in his mother's womb. At breakfast, met
his host & rescuer, Canonicus... (fond friends until the
   end).

The *One* whose contours Boethius explained, & Maximus
evoked. Primordial Spirit, manifest in personal *Three* –
like a Lebanon cedar whose roots emerge from Athens
& Jerusalem. Whose hybrid crown, azure & gold,
condescends to meekest coppery widow's mite... see?
A Lincoln penny – graven in battle for *Equality* (old
name for *Son* & *Providence* alike). & just like us...
your almond glance, *Nadezhda Littletree.* Archangels
   dance.

        *

Last day. This summery September waves goodbye.
Oblomov is calm now, in his rickety octagon.
The air is sweet. He fingers the cardboard icon
of St. Michael. *He will protect you*, she wrote
from Petersburg. Goldfinch flickers by, like a coin
in the fleeting light. A touchpiece? Peter's boat?
The *Sovereign of the Seas* (that incognito sailor ploy
in Amsterdam). There are two sides to everything;
our mongrel binaries are reconciled – by seraph wing.

Even the shimmering *Pantocrator* is always 2-in-1.
That almandine dividing line enkindles freedom
for each child – enlivening implicit human dignity.
No one is king of *Ocean State* : the ultimate sum

of each soul rests beyond the mark of spinning Cain.
So Oblomov meditates his chaste inheritance. The given
is a whispered word... bright & airy as a windblown grain
of sand. The unknown soldier sleeps now, in his grave –
anonymous pebble, silky heir. Green acorn beyond
       gravity).

9.28-30.21

137

This cornucopia of delicate tall grasses, with their wands
of myriad, sand-colored seeds, softly bobbing
beneath October sun. Sweet elegiac flocks
of traveling finches orchestrate their weightless air
of departure. *Lord, don't let me be like lax &*
*indolent Oblomov, snoring beside putrescent pond*s!
I'd rather be in Paradise (George Berkeley's wing).

The young upstart turned his back on London hilarity.
God is not mocked; God visited him everywhere.
Sophistications of the skeleton he could not bear –
his bones ached with that blaze of spiritual charity.

In Paradise (near Newport, by the Berkeley house)
LaFarge flick-flecks one golden lamb, fixed in exactitude
of time, light, weather. George blindly left the *Globe*
& stepped toward his Bermuda stage, lifting an oar
as thespian as any oaken mind might be. Close
by the House of Atreus, the maze of Theseus, the robe
of Ariadne's lightning thread... rosy *parousia* of the Word.

10.4.21

138

October in my airy octagon is really the 10th-month,
mutters oblong ovoid Oblomov to himself. *So sweet*
in spite of that... the perfect month, methinks.
He settles on his crumbling cedar floor, a figure *8*
of infinite travesty. A rusty rooster wind vane creaks.
Birds whistle through the air, seeking Odessa terebinth.

If I cry out, Olga, who might hear me? The Czar?
I will correspond by pigeon, once I know where you are.

The mellow light's already tenuous with winter darkness.
Still fond leaves are dappled for farewell. The drone
you hear is Bach's heart, skipping (cello sarabande).
His *perfect* appears amid boisterous Bruegel mess –
Maria's fleeting smile, creation's merciful caress.
& Hartley's *33* for Hart, from Herman's whalebone
of stark suffering... love is an octahedral diamond
in sand pyramids of pain. Reach through the wilderness.

10.5.21

139

Berkeley in Paradise, motionless, faces the sea.
Nestled beneath the sharp overhang of puddingstone
like a dragon's mouth, or an alligator (peeking
from that emerald cleft north of Newport). The sea
in his mind is not the effervescence of some unknown
formless yet material substrate. It is God's reeking
plot for dolphins, whales – salt matrix of futurity.

Westward the course of Empire takes its way...
That *kingdom come*, not yet arrived, is yet revealed.
By the rude bridge that arched the flood... – say,
does he mean RI? *The denouement's already sealed.*

How can I tell you what I mean, George (Sophie)?
Life's a wave of sonorous quotation. *All the world's
a stage.* The profane chronicles of time are folded
into the tenderest, unfathomable sea-rose destiny –
an origami valentine, wrapped round a rood (*pearls
that were his eyes*). So her cloud-coracle of balsawood
Golgotha skims toward Providence... for you & me.

10.6.21

140

Air growing crisp, days growing short, the seaweed
reek of clammy shoreline muck seeps into town.
That brave magnolia still wavers at the crown
of Observatory Hill (off Hope Street). Shades bleed

toward red, maroon. *The almond is a stubborn thorn.*

Oblomov sleeps, & Berkeley muses, but the Chosen One
reckons the matrix is a horseshoe (wrapped like lead,
like an Iron Crown of Lombardy around his head).
Bees' gold leaven. Mauve petals recollect Redemption.

10.12.21

141

The all-conquering sun sheds fleet October gold,
so delicate & evanescent before winter comes.
Galla Placidia, back in imperial Ravenna, combs
bright straw across the crown of little Valentine.
I travel plain *path P* down to its crossroad rude.
My Providence looms on her seven hills, like Rome's.
Light's empire bruises at its evening rim (green *limes*).

Constantine, sagacious captain, mustered the saints
to make their oath of fealty in Nicene unison.
Ecclesia was militant beneath her exaltation.
Glowing lambs graze tesserae like Seurat paints.

Path P keeps moving, through the times & seasons –
a limb of crooked lightning through the wilderness.
The day after tomorrow, snow will fall; crystalline
star-motes will sprinkle salt into the dying pine.
Thunderheads anchor Byzantium, heeling on wind;
that thorn-oak Empress waits for her double-axe.
Dawn glimmers over Galilee. A kiss remains a kiss.

10.17.21

142

Dry oak leaves almost levitate each pirouette
through ripe October light, slanting their
whimsical, senile farewells toward earth.
All kings are absent-minded fishermen, Musette.

George was a royal dreamer, all right –
sleepwalking to Bermuda. & Oblomov the epicene
aristocrat would make an *O*-ring valentine
her *symbolon* (Olga's icosahedral summer night).

The symbolon's a cryptogram for kingship
as the king's a human crypt of fallibility.
Metaphysical *who*. Riddling creed for *Liberty*
to pose – Gordian knot petulant swords will rip.

Autumn leaves twirl eschatology in semaphore.
In seraph Paradise, oars whisper out to sea.
Redemption came with *Man of Sorrow's* final sigh,
& Restoration is Creation's end – was here before.

10.18.21

143

O sunlight rinsing, brightening the steel crisscross
of your chicken-wire garden, October Hen!
& still we fail to comprehend the enigmatic signage
of these workers, in the graveyard at Gesthemane!
Follow your *path P*, then – lambent dove-message
through dawn's rhodora door – violet sky-vein
pulsing with labor toward one Sabbath metamorphosis!

The axe is laid to the royal oak, a mirror-X –
& from that weary travelers' crossroad
somehow a clean sail lifts & swells... bold
promise of her pilot, Jonah! – to Ocean's matrix.

In the reunion of the manifold Rose
a vast, magnanimous, benevolent sky opens –
over the crown of your skull, an arc of equity
welds its transfiguration through your heart-sea;
& suddenly the wonder of a universe set free
anchors your boughs, ravels the trireme's skeins –
& through the labyrinth of history, honeymilk flows.

10.19.21

144

Berkeley, near Newport, in his puddingstone cave
seated, at rest, on his philosopher's stone
gazed out at the Atlantic (wide glistening azure).
Behind him, the shores of wilderness begin
whose listening gloom unsettles our mythologies.
Local tales... burnished by our own King Dave...
driftwood of feuds, horseshoes, disaster.
The dark forest of the sea beckons to Berkeley
like a constellated *Siris*... like the whole night sky.

& beyond the familiar parochial round, with all
its fancy genealogies – what frames the frames?
He pondered thus, eyes resting on the far horizon.
The kings & queens in London fête their games –
pantomimes of *Royal Oak*; grandiose frivolities;
a micro-urn of Noah's Ark (*Yahweh's Last Call*)...
As if kingship were something absolute for Man.
He thought, *the mind at rest must have its Sabbath day.*
Something rotten in Denmark...? – the thing's a play.

*

The cedar of my body is a rickety gazebo, murmurs
Oblomov (ensconced in wheezing, sighing octagon). Only
a whimsical icon of scriptor Goncharov – whose tours
in frigate *Pallada* were more dismal-baptismal (dipped in
          history).

The numerous origami of Thierry's wholesome chart
is shrouded over many tragic ends – yet there's a breath
of smiling life that governs its geometry. *My heart*
is folded like a valentine, muttered histor Henry at his

death.

& Paradise was where LaFarge brushed his lone lamb
beneath green sunlight (simple, golden, innocent).
Le vitrail vif he guided Henry to adore (blue Miriam);
his fleece was Ariadne's, in her shining puzzle-pavement.

Cinna was murdered by the mob, Navalny threatened
by the Czar – the violence would bear it all away.
But you, dear *dusha-dushka*, limp toward Providence –
pledge of a goldfinch fledged in stone, tombsorrow Day.

                    *

He felt the hollow of his prison cell in the center
of himself, in the pit of his stomach. Boethius
wept salt for his grim fortune, his great fall.
Until, at the dank nadir of midnight, a luminous
apparition of *Sophia* – Wisdom, *per se*, in person –
skimmed through the stones of his own bitter
spirit. She stood before him – dignified, regal,
candid, magnanimous. Boethius took heart.
The Mind, somehow, governs reality – by art.

The cacophony of Babel wakens us each morning
to the drab squabbles of rival dogmatics, like spokes
on a ferris wheel of fortune. & we can't dismount
until we turn & become as little children, folks –
when the small heart palpitates on Halloween
& a lost Pip trembles at the edge of evening;
when every infant spirals to her maelstrom-fount
& Jonah, tossed over, plummets though the whale –
ye whale, *YHWhale*... sky's empty blackness (holy, hale).

In my summer octagon, sometimes the spindly cedar
implicated parallels, enfolded angles. Archangels
of unison made octaves out of figure eights –
& if I shared their vertices with you, these spells
were not in vain. *The well's a-spiral toward the One.*
The *One* perfects *Equality* – bearing its measure,
figuring its image in the matrix of all human fates;
& in the distance you hear music – that *Continuum*
of rock-doves, muted melodies... Creation's hum.

Berkeley, dreaming his puddingstone, tar-water Paradise,
was mocked by rocky objectivists, those solid citizens.
You too, ephebe, are overwhelmed by the abyss –
imagining vast death-dominion, ruled by demons.
But only look now at this face, perfectly human
& divine. This little child will be your friend.
Will take your hand, will lead you upward... kiss
your forehead on the way (to ordinary Providence).
Reality is a moist hearth-sigh – from cosmic happiness.

As all our knowledge is delimited by personhood,
& all our government instilled by phantom royalty
so all our life is grounded in companionship –
& what we know is what *Love* shows us... gradually.
The soul is flaming emerald; heart a living stone –
rotund ruby arrow-eye, circulating Narragansett flood.
This clammy granite you thought salted in death-grip
now traces a gentle curve... soft breast? *Sophie*-canoe?
Dove-wing of *Yeshua* – of *YHWH*, slanting near to you.

*

It's only wind through the dry leaves. Transparent,
rustling. But it makes you want to climb

166

the wooden ladder of these brittle pine limbs
& join the bird-flocks, tumbling beneath gray migrant

clouds. & autumn is an Archimedean well
of otherness, lifted on a point of nothingness –
to be a mirror-fountain, or a drenched sky-sail
that billows from the center of the universe.

& one like Boethius, of restless autumn mind
hungry & athirst for righteousness, discovered Love
& Wisdom in the Word itself : which you too find
already there, buried like a weathered treasure-trove.

Cool autumn wind of exile, pilgrimage! The other side
of Cusa's copper coin – of Thierry's steep-soaring,
interweaving stones. The font of being-born. Wide
eagle-wings, grey dove-plumage... aerial *Taeping*.

*

The philosopher muses, in a philosophical way
about *the One* & *the Many*, *Spirit* & *Time* –
speculative constellations, shrouded by day.
God (incomprehensibly) makes the clocks chime.
Like self-effacing Uncle George (just being himself,
there). Berkeley heeds a more insistent stream.
Spontaneous voice from elsewhere, coursing
evenly through cosmos (rapt in paradisal dream);
comfortable sigh of a child to come, softly nursing.

Like the visionary blind spot, when you missed yourself
in the mirror. Like the mother you took for granted
& the father you never knew – wringing tough pelf
from legal sand (Blackstone, Coke). *The island's haunted,*

Ariel. So you plucked another book from the rocky shelf
of Providence – the one about the *restoration
of all things*. And in those sonorous waves of yarns
brave Penny spun, scrying the end of persecution,
you felt the truth – the way a wobbling lamb learns

(like a drunk) to walk.

10.25.21

145

A chill wind blows through the slats of the gazebo.
My flimsy octagonal microcosm feels worn out.
Autumn's full of premonitions, wayward Hobo-
memories. The voyage homeward's roundabout.
The trireme (in the Mercator projection) hovers
overhead, like *Argo* viewed from Narragansett Bay
sea-floor – heaving *congregations of the Kingdom*
back toward Providence (not very far away). & so
through wintry depths, *Sophia's* keel begins to hum.

Concrete hardscrabble town of Roger Williams, refugee!
Your clever gentry, planted on green promontories
polish colonial brass-rubbings, spars of clipper ships –
your political front, pasted to *pensiones* with glued lips.
Yet meekness covers a multitude of misdemeanors.
Rhode Island, the tiniest microcosm of America –
tardy 13th state, yet *felix* guarantor of Magna Carta;
for *habeas corpus*, Lord Coke's fundamental covenant
certifies both civil liberties – & heavenly government.

October wind rattles these massive oaks on River Road.
The Mississippi snakes on toward the Gulf. My ode
only grows more odious, to the distracted mind
scrolling from cataract to cataract (& going blind).
Redemption Has Already Happened. Prodigal Recovers.
Cribbed headlines furrow the fatal crown of Orpheus.
The Maenads cry – *Eurydice has gone before us.*
Turns toward the lyre, outside RISD Museum...
& turns to stone. Lot's wife (salted for Jerusalem).

Obsessions of the *Golden Bough* circuit their shady oak
interminably. The figure of the Fisher King

recurs, encrypted in his grail (his jail, his joke).
Dry leaves, green acorns. Charles burbles, *everything
will be all right*. Sweet JFK & all his lovers
skim across Newport again, sweep clean the slate.
Camelot lurks amid dark groves of memory
like your Atlantis (plumb beneath *Ocean State*).
Restoration Day, humanity. What will be will be.

10.26.21

146

I may be misconstruing Aristotle, heaven forfend
yet I like the idea. A simple thing, an individual
cannot be classed, or pigeonholed. Each end's
incomprehensibly unique; we lump them all
only by abstractions, paraphrased – which are
not *them*, exactly (distinct, mysterious...
a quiddity). & so when Jesus cited that Jair,
a judge in Israel, whose 30 sons rode 30 asses...

– I don't recall the passage. But when he says
the Son of Man goes as it is determined, I understand
he means the human tribe *in toto*, herd-wise – he
prophesies about us all (squabbling cousins in sand
box). & *when the Son of Man returns again...* here
I sense he designates two things at once – the race
we are, a multitudinous union; & that unique sapphire
or diamond soul (one solitary person's lambent grace).

A monotonous rain here in Minneapolis
is muting the October leaves. Rich scarlet,
umber, yellow-gold. There will be days like this.
The garbage men collect wet bags of torn leaflets,
my scraps of untranslated incunabula (a word I had
forgot just now). & *are we written in the Book of Life?*
Nicholas collected scrolls, gleaned from that dead
hive around *Hagia Sophia* – his sole joy, his only wife.

& Providence? Still over there, to the east,
shrouded in rainclouds off the coast. I remember
dark hair, dark eyes... stray glimpses at most.
Your painful grin, your slightly bitter laughter –
faint survivals, immemorial innocence.

Reliquary of seashells, dry seaweed's tang.
& when the *Son of Man* flares... your calm affluence
of cosmic sunshine – keys the Seven Sisters sang.

10.28.21

147

Take a deep breath of sharp cool autumn air.
Like these bold red-gold maples across the street
at the Masonic Brain Science Center – breathing,
swirling, oscillating in their opalescent light (replete
with ripening). October slants toward Halloween,
shining. When the rude body & the spirit share
a suddenly uncanny urge to levitate (what haunting
sense). Jerusalem artichokes wither to transience. Yet
still their spindly stalks, bedizened, stay... to dance.

Like those anonymous masons at Chartres, or Thebes
I want to articulate the speechless frame of things –
just as quaint gestures of a poem, or a mime
suggest unspoken moods behind our posturings
to calibrate the underlying ground of our good will.
Not to impose my own belief, but to hypothesize
the scaffolding of possible happiness – to rhyme
heart's intuition with my brain-fed burble of realities
& seek that pyramidal pedestal of *Liberty*, ephebes.

You must become an ignorant child again,
where voyages begin. By the shore of *Ocean
River*, amid a misty spume of sparkling galaxies.
At the moss-point end of *Paradise*, where Berkeley's
meditation lifted him unto his smiling *Ark*-angel...
the teeming crown of life. *Love* is the root of happiness,
& happiness the strength of families, towns, nations;
Love the source of all that equanimity, that stations
guards around its children – lifts the hungry to its nest.

When I was young, I crossed the Red Sea into Israel.
I passed into the *Ocean State*, I rode a conch shell

into microcosmic Providence. I piled up sin,
& fell into the retrograde nightmare of Everyman
until a dove-like *Jonah* rescued me from jail – again.
I felt an oak-leaf crown around my head... reborn.
An infant (like a swelling *mandorla* of joy & adoration)
I watched *Benevolence* poured out, across Creation...
grasped the *Charter* of our liberty (green-gold acorn).

10.29.21

148

Of all the ghosts that gather this time of year
there is one Ghost, beyond all the rest.
Like *Hagia Sophia with a million eyes*, her nest
of *glossolalia* glazes every ark, globes every sphere.
How to write that ship, like a talisman... an oracle
with a capital C? Like Black Elk's rood of rectitude :
a 3-dimensional crossroad, beaming *neighborhood* –
enfolded in a sea-rose valentine (your paper coracle).

It is no encrypted shibboleth of knowledge, then –
the model ship unfolds bare *justicemercy* (heartbroken).

& to right the ship? In the eye of hurricane
off the coast of Rhode Island – where one will
for *liberty of conscience* anchors *Constitution*, still.
Where sea-bells echo a covenant made plain –
*to love the Lord your God, & love your neighbor
as yourself.* This simple matrix of the mast & keel
is like that child, afloat with acorns & oak-gall...
our once & future human crown (Love's living heir).

10.30.21

149

This fleet of golden, calm & mild October days
glides slowly into its gray winter harbor. Weather
like this might inculcate us with such moderation –
instill a lesson (about equanimity, forbearance,
& the path of peace). The rules we keep by force
are only figures for a more pervasive breeze
of mutual awareness, our instinctual dance
of natural law – brash extremes held by a tether
of humility (wisdom's beloved comrade, sister, twin).

& then the last act of October, in her burnished armor
is an apotheosis of this ripening light – the breaking-in
of another sense of time & stillness. The tentative,
silent footsteps... leafy shades in solemn procession;
the memory of dear ones, utterly beyond our reach.
Today, in a forgotten cupboard, hidden by my mother
long ago, I found an ancient delicate red-brown basket
shaped like a pumpkin – & inside, a simple amulet
collection, from Jerusalem. *Seek ye the Lord & live.*

A plastic bag, holding small nondescript stones
(from Galilee?). Little shards of pavement, pottery.
A thin bent strip of iron, the size of a stamp –
with a cutout of a tiny square cross, full of empty
light. Grant thy departed peace, O Lord, we beseech
thee. *O Jerusalem, how I would gather you, like a hen
gathers her brood about her... if only you would know
the ways that make for peace*! Boethius, in his clamp
of iron, loved *Wisdom* as his very quickness, here below.

The exaltation of the high number, weight & measure
manifest in the vault of Chartres' massive stones!

That *claritas*, *integritas*, & *consonantia* of things
bears witness to wholeness, hefting this rondure
like a diadem of galaxies, tracing their vast course –
a living spirit, ineffable intelligence, nursing our sense
of personhood within a more substantial personhood
we can but project – beyond the border death brings,
finally, to our dear friends. Love's doorway, world.

10.31.21

150

November brings another mood. Changeable skies,
restless clouds. Like an old man's thought.
Like the shady obverse of a copper penny – Cusa's
twilight *imago*. Morse code... *what hath God wrought?*
– on the Day of the Dead. The heart grows lonely,
prone to desolation blues. When the hearth burns
low, & thin birds rattle chuttering around their tree,
& Isis searches everywhere for dead Osiris (yearns).

Oblomov in his rickety gazebo mooned for Olga, so.
St. Valentine & Boethius both felt that gnawing need
to assuage love-melancholy – longed for a friend.
The human heart is naturally affectionate, Dante (solo)
underlined, in his vernacular. Man is *animale
compagnevole*, toto *simpatico*. Will write wild Jael
from his jail – send jokes to good-time Royal Charlie
hiding out in her pretender's oak (acorn, be well).

*

So the snowtime approaches. When the dry hexagons
skitter across each chilly pavement snare, frozen.
All strive unthinkingly toward warmth – sons,
daughters, uncles, grandmothers... earth-children.
The gravity of clay moves an old fool more slowly.
The *Día de Muertos*, like a ring in his pocket – see?
A book of matches, set beside him in his grave,
must trim the candle of his lust (O hollow knave).

Someone placed a few stones atop the marble
of your mother's monument. Not in Jerusalem,
but in Swan Point – where two circles interwhelm

like a still pair of dancers, arched, immoveable.
On my father's birthday (king of anonymity,
unknown soldier... baron of meekness).
The goldfinch loses his own gold to frost, annually –
but your love burns like bronze... heals all distress.

11.1.21

151

Two gardeners (yardmen at the Brain Science Center,
across the street) are draining the water pipes
for winter, releasing an evanescent fountain spray;
a willowy sunlit water-veil, beneath an array
of three young autumn trees (orange, scarlet, gold).
But where oh where is that well of living water,
the forest spring of high *Sophia* – lifting our hopes
to everlasting life? Boethius in prison, Berkeley
dreaming on his rock in Paradise... enthuse with me.

The science in *my* brain... swampland of memory,
projected on a plan of Providence. Not my own,
but Maxwell's Maytime diorama. Of a seacoast city –
gray & convoluted as limestone *matière de Bretagne*;
austere, bewildered as gold labyrinth of Chartres.
There is that emerald seaweed whiff of Camelot –
rose-tinted ideal Kennedy, the once & future king;
& that Cusa *coniunctio* – a thorny Roger, prophet
of *soul liberty*, & thronèd Charlie (*Rhody*-chartering)...

& yet... *It was not price nor money could have purchased
Rhode Island; Rhode Island was purchased by* LOVE.
Like some magnetic motherlode of iron, you coalesce
my rejected *disjecta membra* (ala Dürer's *Melencolia*)
into a formula of shipwright's ark, or *Argo* manifold –
into the pattern of an evergreen, humane *ecclesia*
which rises billowing from ghoulish mariner's business
like a child's airship of Galilee (its pilot beaming far above)

*   *   *

The soldering iron of experience refines gray matter

& the molten heart, melds them as two-in-one.
Like silver gondolas of Providence, knotted, woven
with wild violets & shoreline roses of the *Ocean State*.
To trace the *Ariadne*-memory of love is all my art.
Following one almond-shaped goldfinch – down a path
laid out beforehand. By our hybrid, mongrel paragon
of all reunions, weddings… restoration, reconciliation.
Your blooded crown with diamond diadem, *Lord Sabaoth*.

11.2.21

PART THREE

152

Your sense of color seeps into the sketch you made.
With your small right hand, with your innocence.
All our scribbled scripture is umbilical, after all –
Daniel's, Dante's. Dadda, dreaming back to spring.

To the soulful source of those four rivers of Hell –
a splintered statue full of tears. With golden mind
& silver-mirroring, wave-tremulous heart; intestines
of ambivalent, amenable copper; thighs of turbid
envious bronze; stiff iron legs, & two uneven troubled
feet (one talon of steel – one painfully hobbled
foot of clay). Held together by waves, erupting again.

Yesterday the maple leaves, like a flood of tears
went tumbling from black limbs. Twilight sun-yellow
more golden than gold. Like a Lincoln penny
fate turned our misshapen compromise of law spinning
like a gyroscope across one thin lifegiving memory.
It was your weaver-lamb's rose labyrinth – it was
Ariadne's rescue (almond bark for Daniel's river-flow).

11.8.21

153

The wash of syllables on the strand of the *Sea of Agape*,
that is poetry. & your dream of the *Ocean State*
is like an ur-charter of *Lovingkindness* – to create.
Thus *Genesis* was but the preamble to Act Three
in *The Comedy of Providence* – enacting an encounter
between all-unready *Everyman* & utterly uncanny
Numinous. That's what the Bible means to me.
(*Discuss with Sheba – what it means to her.*)

Once upon a time, a tiny impolitic colony was planted
by the bleak Atlantic seashore, between Boston &
New Haven – betwixt hubristic, scientismic speculation
& mesmeric mantras (of a fundamentalist persuasion).
Roger Williams called it *Providence*, in holy gratitude
for that benevolent nod of assent, that *annuit coeptis* –
midwived by gentle Narragansett chief Canonicus
out of one frigid blizzard of exile. Humane beatitude.

11.9.21

154

November wheels on its raspy spoke of evening gloom.
A chariot, troubling the querulous dry leaves.
Deracinated wrath creaks back & forth
when men have traded off the bread of life
for something promising, near-at-hand (sheaves
of mirage). *Nobody of it is worth.*
The riders, riders! Bronze heralds of doom.

The leaves are like embodiments of leaven-yeast.
Almost human. Ink dries beneath eyelids
of mummified scribes. All those royal deeds!
But who is this bold lamb, skippering from the East?

The shiver up your spine – only an echo of encounter.
Monarch metamorphosis; the restoration of your
self. Flesh cannot inherit the eternal kingdom,
child – only SPIRIT lifts you from this chafing strife
of blind men, badgering each other blind. *O hear,
Israel*! Eternity, unfolding. To the zither-strum
of fellowship... forecast of almond petal-shower!

11.10.21

155

Dark sky the color of gray stone. A migrant wind
that seems to sail hunched leaves through my heart.
Thought of Apollinaire in his gray capital (a wounded
veteran). Bruised martins cloister in an old rampart.

Wars to end all wars against ourselves will end as well.

Life grows simpler in cold & winter – crystallized
like salt, or sleet. *Let your yes be yes, & your no
be no*. Lincoln was every veteran's father. Revised
the laws to harmonize conscience – tuned Union, so.

11.11.21

156

Gleaning their last gold against November slate
the veinèd chalices of ancient maples, like
those gnarled fingers of your potter-mother
shed blasons of the sun (phosphorous counterpoint).
& when the wool skeins that bind us to each other
suddenly fray & break... when life's lightning-strikes
bolt us to mourning – *still shalt thou love, not hate.*

The meek brown penny, smallest of all coins
was once pervasive through these States (a single
cent). The copper spine of a slow serpent joins
each flickering riverbend... embers of *Ocean* mingle.

What you remember is that engraved profile – gaunt,
smiling. Leaning down, benevolent – always there
already. Like the father you never knew – like Mike
(your brother) nicking fire from sky, for this joint.
The red flame scattered (from the brain) like quick
lightning – like flickering palms around a potter's urn.
Humming, ready (in your veins). For a shepherd's hunt.

11.12.21

157

A tentative first snow outlines the shapes of things,
like my mother's imponderable, hieratic paintings
of the 70's. Edged with mute gold – transposing figures
of forked branches, lounging Lake Nokomis dreamers.

Outlines haunt each object, like a metaphysical blessing.
Commingled hexagons – *continua* of river-crystal.
Maximus felt light stings slant through his prison cell.
& Boethius, in Pavia... axles of mind's misunderstanding.

Turn, turn, old rigid Glasgow statue of concrete.
Your unspent tears already fill the Earth with white.
L'uomo naturalmente e compagnevole animale.
     Conversation
aids the mind – mind informs heart. *Intelletto d'amore*

guides us to that Restoration that is always there –
Redemption, seeping through our bones, beyond our
broken minds to comprehend. *Agape* (simple,
powerful). Undying paradigm; unbreakable example.

11.13.21

158

Lateness coming early in autumn, & the low sun
drawing close behind a mottled silver sky, looking in
like a flicker of blaze in the hearth at harvest time,
& the long hallways of lonesome avenues, gilded
now with muttering leaves, seem to swell one theme
like an insect orchestra tuning up toward unison
when the shrill pipe of *all hands on deck* is sharply blown

& all the masses of people, & all their manifold doings
under the hulking shell of anxious, vigilant demands –
their laws, like thick rhinoceros skin pushing through
        sands
gnarled & heavy as oak trunks (pecked by bee-stings)...

& you sense the gathering force of all this harvesting
& you note the remote concord between distant times
when the union of prudence & benevolence (one high
Sophia radiating through these autumn clouds) welded
the rooted equity of Edward Coke, & Roger Williams'
liberty of conscience, & Lincoln's meek & merciful penny
to the firm tenor of MLK – a rebuilt *Constitution*,
        harboring.

11.14.21

159

November. Light of a foreshortened sun, days
quickening toward evening. Time runs at its end,
slowly. The pace of a spun planet none can mend,
bent on its ecliptic – wobbly, wheezing through haze.

The earth with its inhabitants (enemies, neighbors)
is like a cracked & fatal Round Table – wounded
by vertigo, afflicted by mistrust. Each Mordred
& Arthur, each Guinevere & Lancelot, prepares

for their own solitary grave. Is there a spirit
of a people? Is there a unity of purpose? Soul?
Like *Liberty*, majestic statue in the harbor – whole
& calm, wise & full of grace? Lifting her light?

Or is it rather *Old Ironsides*, or that *San Pablo*
sounding some fickle channel of the Yangtze?
Stubby, *blocky*, *topheavy*, *& all moonwhite*, she –
but like a cozy veteran's home, for Holman. *Yo* –

Paper Jake Holman! Unknown sailor! Suffering
across the globe, in every war... devised by men
for their own petty pride & brutal avarice. Amen.
We've all gone searching for the Grail – something

glittering there, under the stones of our own tomb.
Jack Kennedy was just another Holman, too.
The drums rattle, off in the distance. Cold blue
heavens overhead. Irrevocable now (Fate's loom).

The artist, canvas toward Thanksgiving, dreams
of a reunion. Of the Many & the One – the family

& your enfolded heart's icon. Even (eventually?)
bruised red-&-blues of Byzantine cathedral schemes.

My mother's ancient backyard morning scene
glows in the kitchen – quiet, vibrant, early green.
A flock of blackbirds reaps the grass (between
a neighbor's blue garage, those oaks' blithe sheen).

A principle of Unity absorbed the fractious Greeks.
The pre-Socratic function of the One (its name
debatable) was that credo controlling every game;
sagacity was high *Sophia* – rightness every city seeks.

Green bird's-eye view by Maxwell Mays, of Providence.
Only a synthesis of tiny details, only an abstract
of a microcosm... infinity of local myth, in fact.
Each brush-stroke like a snowtrack on the immense

ice-monument of mind's sullen paralysis, heart's
frozen *caritas*. A child sweeps angel-wings
across hard stubble... these my evanescent mornings
swerve back through the mirror of Rhode Island (art's

light breathing on the chill, impersonal glass)
& measure my feeble mediocrities... parochial
mile past village mile of memories. Your smile,
slighted Penelope; your courage, comely sweetness,

copper-wire Penny, spinning Jenny. Like a pebble
in the river-sand (uncounted, unaccountable).
Yet *Imago* (like Imogen, Cordelia). & from the fable
of the ocean, steps the heroine herself – my treble
                              C.

193

Magnanimous, omni-octagonal *Hagia Sophia*
stands for the omnipresent *Imago* made flesh –
one who rises from laborious villages, to mesh
with God & neighbor. *Agape* (firm, whole). Jonah

as mourning dove, cooing from cornice in Byzantium

emerges from that grey whale in your heart.
Grey as November sky, Rhode Island stone.
Hidden like a pebble on wavebeat shoreline
one cloudy day, calling – *come friend, take part.*

                    A
round here is round everywhere. Hear, hear!
With your ear, O hearty earth. & with your mind,
ambitious, enterprising hand – don't clench unkind.
For the loss is dear; your soul is all that matters

here. Integral, whole – flowering. The sweep
of constellations, through the mantle of the Bear
cups each with awe. *Wain of Charles*, there –
woven like sails, masted to majesty of night. Steep

light. Just so the Hound of Heaven's coming back
(sound, waving). You touch a universal chord,
Maxwell (*Maximus*, chanting through shackles). Lord,
liberate us from our own decrepitude – let slack

your wrath. The table of Thanksgiving is forlorn,
& we who gather everything from Earth
feud with each other. Spiteful mirth – mirth,
murk – dearth, dirk – mourn, mourn...

obfuscate. For the tub glides, down the Yangtze;

everyone survives – the missionaries, revolutionaries...
everyone (except inconsequential Holman). Seize
the day, scryptographers! It is the slippery story of *glory*.

I don't know how it lasts, how it sustains –
the thread of Ariadne (through the ages, through
the years). Beyond the labyrinth of self-division, O...
dread *Minotaur* of mirrors (feral blindness it contains).

Only a continuum of *One* fulfills thy Promise thus,
in equal Persons – one beyond the number one.
A marriage of sweet *Agape* with each & all, soon,
soon – uniting everyone at last (in lovingkindness).

Over the turbid chaos of the hungry crowd
light travels up the railroad tracks. At the end
of *State Fair* (at the beginning of the end).
It is the beckoning torch of *Liberty*... pellucid

node of spiritual clarity. Lamp for people
struggling like sheep, to find a pasture gate.
We are no longer subject to the diktat
of tyrannical fate, like wistful Constantinople...

we do not have to be resigned. *Your conscience
is potential ally of good will*, ponders Roger;
what you believe – CHRISTRUTH – *is word to which
        your*
heart gives right consent... your mind adjudges sustenance.

Alleluiah. That is the truth – & Truth
is who we seek. *Transparent air...* deep
breathing trust. Uncommon good (our

own to keep). From husk of wayward Ruth

a goldenrod, like Aaron's staff, aboard a river
pontoon. Nubian canoe, Petersburg barge...
transmuting *unknown soldier*, still at large;
molting a chrysalis of kingship (*shiver*).

The muse resides inside an oak, according to
The Golden Bough – I don't know how. Ariel,
bring me to your Promised Land. America, I'll
hoot the harmony IONA yodels me (*you-who*).

11.15-16.21

160

A strong cold wind blows through the leafless branches.
Leaves scratch along the street, like orphan scribes
scribbling obscure last chronicles of roving tribes.
Hands wither to the task. The heart blanches

beneath shrouded November light, keeling hard
across dark winter waves. To seek that clarity
which correlates random phenomena, & see
the *telos* of the whole – within the scrambled herd

of nicked & tottering deflections. Bare oak limbs
climb through outlines of a three-master. The lifting
verticals, intrepid prow – like a conducting
rod, prompting the keel (humming sea-hymns)...

The *Providence*, *Old Ironsides*, the *Constitution*.
How mingle these fog-shrouded shapes – these
hollow acorn-coracles (lightweight) drifting sideways
across my *Ocean River* of confusion? & summon

a simple, intellectual trireme – elegant model
for potential voyage? Like *Pallada's* (a planetary
circumnavigation)? Must not be purely literary...
maybe charismatic? Like the liminal parallel

of Nicholas of Cusa's *coniunctio oppositorum*... or
how the equilibrium of Roger Williams' dual tables
of the Law (sacred & secular domains) enables
flourishing sovereign civility. O rightful freedom!

The mind hungers with fearsome natural appetite
for the intellectual sustenance of truth. For wisdom,

high *Sophia*. But the heart is difficult to plumb...
its *charism* – unquenchable AGAPE (soul's deep delight).

Black Elk stood on the rise of desolate autumn prairie.
Mutely lifted his pipe, to signify the six directions.
Pythagoras adumbrated an order of *Numeros* – One's
a number ante number; intangible points align geometry

of universal unity. Sweet mathematics! So the mind
exults in blustery clear air – blasting so cold
across a solar panoply of orbiting comet-mold!
Bruno was burned for this, his cosmos left behind;

yet integral union of all manifest phenomena
is part of every heart's dream of reality.
It is the hope of reconciliation, of the *I*
with Thou; it is the limping gait of sweet Natasha

walking along beside Osip, Nadezhda... *gentle*,
gentle. Do not ruffle the waters of your soul,
Grace, Ariadne. *Flowers are immortal; heaven
is whole*. Almond is blooming (on a limb-spindle).

That pivotal *kairos* in this world, when the *Word*
goes inward (piercing to marrow). Heart
thirsts for an echo for its adoration. Chartres
evocation – lofty space beneath the stars. A bird

plummets from the constellation of your Face,
belovèd; Sheba, your companion in wisdom
traveled from far Ethiopia to know its sum.
Love is creation's mantle – planet's grace.

America, you are indeed a cosmos – not from within,
but from without. Not from yourself, but *Wakan Tanka*
(Great Spirit). Not for the bitter rich, but (*alleluiah*)
for blithe children of the poor. This crown –

I double you, acorn : like octahedral diamond

gleaming in lichen-copper crown. *Divine & human
joinèd, without separation or confusion* – like a Lincoln
penny (flicker in afflicted trench). Face of someone
warm, beloved – wise, benevolent (black-eyed Susan).

*

Wistful November. Month of loss, & Armistice,
& harvest thankfulness. Beneath the slanting leaves
& plummet of dusk – the year's twilight. Heaves
a sigh, gathers in the tribes... against the malice

of mere force, falsehoods of treacherous impunity;
all those malignant threats to this free commonweal
of human sovereignty, of human dignity... her seal
printed in crimson wax (bees' realm of liberty).

My simple numbers would sketch out an ancient
metaphysical geometry; a framework of enfolded
& unfolding differences, inside a maximum, dead-
centered, infinite, unparaphrasable & cognizant

Presence. The *Shekinah* (one lambent, ambient
benevolence, beyond our ken). *Thou knowest,
Lord.* How the *One-not-one* unfolds the sweetest

199

measure (in a bounded universe) of love's intent;

giving unto the dying flesh the vital crosscurrent
of countervailing & divine (spontaneous) kindling.
The rustic, wooden rood of love's just *even-ing*.
So *loving God & loving neighbor* prove – equivalent.

Black Elk enacts his navigation of the covenant
standing in a vast ocean of forsaken plains
like a stone fallen from heaven, like a man in pain.
No one will judge. Loving mother, father most decent...

generous, magnanimous, blessedly loving-kind.
Inexpressible fullness of personal donation (*agape*).
These striving people who came before show me
the proof of Osip's, Oscar's savory tamarind :

divine Redemption, children, has already happened.
The clarity & probity of simple justice mirrors
the veteran rightness of Boethius – just so Thierry's
scintillating Chartrian topology rotates our happy end

to our beginning (O embattled & afflicted human being).
& Nicholas (that shining, coruscating brilliant star,
that warm, incomprehensible *Mars-Venus* avatar)
devised a game for us to play : *De Ludo Globi* (singing

Game of Spheres). The most profound & droning
B-fiat, at center of this black-hole universe...
grave *Gravity King* of multitudinous *Deep Space* –
we roll these skewed footballs toward your last inning

(ridiculous balloons, pumpkins...). It's only us.

US – human tops, spinning like egocentric knights
around a Round Table already fractured (at least
twice). Yet I sense a restoration (happy endlessness).

If *the Redemption has already happened* (Acmeist
poets in Petersburg held firmly to this faith
against a swarm of envious, inhuman wrath)
Bulgakov's humorous satire might still insist –

the grace of human equilibrium is indestructible.
It is the SPIRIT that gives life; the flesh
is of no avail. & they will smile up there (wraith-
wingèd friends)… where Thanksgiving is indelible.

11.19-20.21

161

Chill wind chases off the last remnants of autumn.
Evening sky at the horizon, like a memory of rainbow –
opalescent blue, mauve, violet & pink shadow
late filaments of gold. Light's cup brims solemn

family covenant : *Adieu, adieu, remember me.*
The Goulds watched over Newport Synagogue
for years (caretakers, Quaker friends). *Gog*
& Magog shall not uproot inheritance of Zebedee

where George, the President, vowed fellowship
& safety in the land, for every uptorn refugee.
That it might be, that it might always be!
Union is natural as bliss – as Whitman's *mothership,*

America. Your poets, idiots & holy fools proclaim
the same – a crazy innocence (mad north-northwest).
Infant beatitude & gruesome horror interlaced
bind our inheritance; vengeance, pathos, shame

rise from a deep-sown yeast of wrath. The iron
seed of violence, hail of malevolence against
those *others* – neighbors, strangers... rival agents
in a prestidigitation of power, dominion. *My son,*

my son... remember me. Through arid cyberspace
invisible pellets of deceptive vipers permeate –
treason, division, callousness... fear, contempt
& hate. So we are dehumanized in our disgrace.

O stark wind of providential wrath! *The judgements*
of the Lord are true & righteous altogether, keened

the Psalmist in his woe, shaken by the fiend
of war. *There's a divinity that shapes our ends,*

rough hew them how we will (whispered the resolute
rail-splitter to himself). *The arc of the moral universe
is long, but it bends toward justice,* murmured the martyr's
hopeful heart. So let their magnanimity take root!

We are like carousers at the Round Table, reeling
away, astray... into an empty nightmare of alienation,
a travesty. Satanic betrayal of ourselves, our nation,
our own neighbors. & wrath is a hurricane, wheeling...

verily, *they who sow the wind, shall reap the whirlwind.*
We chose the sniper's means to overthrow the king –
the hunter's .22, for bringing down the deer (walking
Green Mountains). & so the same against each kind

of enemy, each stranger – every other tribe we felt
as only rivalry, or danger; so the cold autumn wind
swings round, against ourselves. *So do not send
to ask, for whom the bell tolls.* Sonorous iron will melt

your own hearts, then. *Johnny, we hardly knew ye!*
Our own charmed son, our chosen one, our prince
is suddenly stricken – shattered! Swept from hence
in the blink of an eye – the welling of a tear... ay me!

The ghastly absurdity of our scene is perfect nausea;
the pathos in Dallas, vulnerable people standing by...
our human flesh so fragile, palpable – compelled to die!
We are imprisoned by the force of our own wrath. *Selah.*

*

George... & Charles... those old English kings
drowsing in the oaklands of a borrowed royal robe.
The patient unction of a loyal people, at *the Globe*
or under sparse moor-thatch (with hunger pangs).

A wedding barge glides down the rippling Thames

& so the dream of Everyman floats on the breeze.
A monarch feints & zigzags through the shade
where grace is manifest in light, not made by
hands. The sun (a penny) glints between the trees.

*

My mind luffs like a jib in a shifty wind. Ballast
I need; I scavenge what I can. Thierry of Chartres
shaped a fourfold metaphysics – simple numbers
in reciprocal tension, like tightrope of a gymnast

knots the lofty determinate providence of *One*
into the depths of a jumbled, sliding hold
of chance – of *Multitude* – of possibility. A fold
for Grace to show her hand. Felt (woolen-spun)

into an origami Rose – each mauve, overlapping
petal edged as sharp, precise & scintillating
as *beryllonitrine* – Cusa's glittering scarlet ring,
clothed in mossy copper leaves (aslant, whirling).

Henry Adams absorbed the tidal, magnetic undertow
of the Queen of Heaven, there. Soft light
through fountains of rainbow glass. Her might,
her unearthly gravity, drew John LaFarge, also –

crossing the sea-rose streams of *Ocean*, into Paradise.
Where solitary Berkeley meditated God's design –
a palimpsest of dream-Bermudas (spun more fine
than dew-strung spiderwebs, or peacock's eyes).

The mind, through storms, must find its calm compass.
Wisdom is like a contra-dance, or sarabande, of keel
& rudder; both submerged, unseen – & yet we feel
that gentle, whelming rightness. Ineffable windlass

anchoring our heart to life's wholeness, our spirit
to the consecration of all things unto each other –
*Lord, your fields & pastures... O immense mother
Earth...* your salt necessity inwoven with a

serenity. Inevitable truth bound up with justice
like an anchor for the hoped-for future – all things
singing & laboring together, up the everlasting rungs
of schooner *Providence* (from port to shore, miraculous).

Only turn, Humanity, from petty hate, self-serving treason;
turn your face toward that *Ocean* of benevolence
whence all things come... ineffable Providence,
Sophia's wisdom-sense. It is the Source, divine-human,

Who is the matrix of the elegant *Game of Spheres* –
a golden lamb at the foundation of the labyrinth
of breeze-enlivened sea-roses. A minuscule ninth
Pip – between two decks, & thirteen cruel colonies –

a simple point, a turning-point (your soul's pivot).
As when Hamlet, bound (bound) for London
finds his father's blood-wax seal... & so treason

is yet undone – his resolution yet redeems the plot;

so every simple trembling soul might encounter You
someday... before the end of time. O Thou
whose good will helps us mirror thee, & speed the plow
past each piratical *Jolly Roger*, to an *Ark* made new –

bestow upon us grateful hearts; provide our ship
with such calm measure of kindness & charity
to make our harvest one of concord, magnanimity –
dream grail-vessel (our commonweal your fellowship).

11.22-24.21

162

At the end of November, at the low end of the year
Earth mimes the desolation of an old man's heart.
Yet the river flows on calmly, plays her part
beneath barren cottonwoods. Carries his bier.

Advent will bring another child into the world.
Someone with a simpler, more courageous way.
Always looking for the good, not how to get away
with improvised effronteries (convenient yield).

Your birthday, disaffected Ariadne, sad Penelope.
A disenchanted Henry slowly ambulates the maze
at Notre Dame – where frozen Theseus will gaze
forever, trapped in the weft of his own perfidy.

He twists a 4-leaf clover in his fingers, absently
(misapprehended microcosm, skewed mandala).
Lance of a sundial casts revolving shade, *selah*...
the sun is low. A mourning dove must rescue me.

*

Poetry is in some sense naked speech.
Simple, the simplest. A cube of salt.
Excruciating truth (brings time to halt).
Into your heart & soul the Word will reach.

& there are sidelong things to learn from this
about reality itself. It is (to a degree) a dream.
It is your soul – working out its devious theme,
its fractured scheme. It is your paradigm of bliss

& torment – it is your confrontation with yourself.
But not yourself : for the Ghost on the ramparts
of the castle garden shatters all your arts
& sciences, Henry. She is the shadow of the Gulf

of Mexico; she is the whorl of Ariadne's spindle
lifted into thundercloud (brain-matter *de Bretagne*);
she is the whale who swallowed your companion
Jonah (dove still floating from your birth-canal).

Like trees, walking! exclaimed the healed blind man
observing (for the first time) human beings.
Poetry, birth-lump of clay the Rabbi brings –
bird-flute that kindles us to dance (back to reunion).

*

Forever there is a touch of flummery about kingship.
The lordly one, amid counselors (according to Hocart)
was only inches from the scapegoat's tumbrel cart.
Bureaucracy was camouflage (give 'em the slip).

His face on the coin was useful for exchange –
& if the drought lingered, the coin was lightweight
& the king was dead. Long live Hubert the Great!
Soul liberty (writ Williams) is the sign of God's image,

raying out from each person. Into an anxious dream
of human flocks, their indispensable shepherds –
these crowds, tossed in the wind of frenzied words.
I cannot contrive to correct my kingship scheme.

A lethal conundrum – immemorial entanglement
with mass menace (hysteria, delusion, violence).

208

Only the gratuitous gift of supernatural *caritas*
may wake us from our manacled sleepwalker's bent.

*

Cloud-shallops emigrate across far winter blue.
A buffeting wind soon floats the snowflakes,
unevenly rimes each shape a mouth makes.
Mayflower, rose-petal, pennyroyal (balm for you).

how waves of sky tack sails athwart this island road

Families gather in their houseboats full of ghosts.
Pilgrims were travelers, settlers were refugees.
The nakedness of animals; harsh cold breeze.
A dolphin washes up at midnight. Crosstrees, masts.

*

Dawn light strengthens as the slow sun inches round.
December brings a quiet clarity; the year resigns.
Hope for an offspring yet, beyond this pale... signs
echo from our familiar well. Wool knots are bound.

Intelligence is master of the Earth, ephebe.
Old subtle Coke, the man of law, & providential
zealous Williams, haughty devious Founders – all
recognized the dialect, the *telos* of our happy globe.

Power of self-governance; the humane possibility
of civil rule. By reason of the true, the just.
Plain equilibrium of species-equity (space dust
to dust). Just so *Sophia* reigns – statutes of Liberty.

Yet poets' words are paltry to portray the whole.
Tentative light, filtering through bare branches...
its rhythm of diaphanous bird-heart launches
Ironsides. A faded goldfinch tunes the next chorale.

                              *

These quiet giant cottonwoods, bending toward the sun
above the riverbank – a sun itself barely able to rise
over the south ridge, opposite – would not suffice
for mast or mainstay. This posthumous season

dead limbs & leaves are feast for humus & fungi;
black char-cushions, threaded with rhizome spores,
frosted spiderwebs – below disintegrating doors
of roving clouds – accompany the afterlife of *you-&-I.*

The past returns over the brow of the hill, on the edge
of the redoubt, on the castle wall. A gray bird coos
& murmurs there, calls you & me – out of the blues,
out of the reds (out of the pale green lichen, sedge).

The Word burns on the poet's lips – oxidizes, buzzing
like larval wasps in the oak-gall. Transmutations
out of mesmerized paralysis – fathers & sons
breaking the royal seal. Hamlet reversed, returning

to Elsinore – to right the ship, to undo tyranny.
A dove yodels at the edge of Advent, in December.
Jonah's breathing, underwater. & you remember
a faded mottled valentine, from Providence (*FT*).

                              *

210

Six months from now, on the diagonal from here
where the year dies its bleak lonesome death
on the way to being born (outside Nazareth
maybe, or Galilee) Rhode Island is emerald sphere

or *Bird's-Eye View of Providence*, by Maxwell Mays.
& your *Mayflower* is an enormous rose in our eye
& *The Once & Future King* a humble garbage guy
in Atlanta. & then we're dazzled by plupurple dais,

violet haze (topsy-turvy foolish feast, of abject
Unknown Soldier glory). Lincoln riding on a train,
back to anonymous prairie grave – his copper coin
of the realm gone absent. Absinthe, green (perfect).

You fold your paper *Mayflower* into a valentine.
The *Ocean State* is sighing, somber (wave on wave).
The crown blossoms into an acorn ship (your grave).
The king is in his coracle; his silky horse is *Columbine*.

11.27-12.1.21

163

A fierce wind under muted sky. The year's first snow
scatters in sudden flocks of mist. It's colder now
in Afghanistan. A family fades out, in flimsy tent.
If this was right, it's not what anybody meant.

Le vent souffle. Le chemin, la route, the way.
Translate *suffering* – reverberates to Judgement Day.
Where there's money to make, the inns are full.
We know what's right, but the cold have pull.

We know what's right. Love is our natural law.
There from the beginning, spake the calm rabbi –
he smiles, he wears an acorn on his ear. He
doesn't die. He hugs a sheep. The wind is raw.

Over the oceans come the pilgrim waves
suffused with salt, the way snow rims caves.
Cave whispers to Coke, to Roger Williams –
that sea of stars still bears your righteous hymns.

12.5.21

164

Jupiter floats above languorous Luna tonight
like power over curved reflection.
December air is cold & clear. The sun
is on the other side of Earth. *More light,*

more light. Imogen outlived her enemies,
but that was only in a play. Roger Williams
was a refugee. We are all microcosms
of a *Paraclete* – shifted on a pilot breeze.

If *God is Love...* love flies out from itself,
toward that which you adore. Its constancy
a steadfast capability (Keats felt, you see)
strong as death... cruel as the grave.

But Jupiter is jovial, *vraiment*? Magnanimous,
generous – like Bloom in crabby, pinchback
Dublin. No? *Mais oui.* Like Villon on the rack –
like Mary Magdalen (heartbroken, shedding tears).

You have entered a Narragansett conversation,
Roger, that began before you arrived. *Before
all things were made* – that is canonical, my dear
Canonicus. & so we ramble toward a restoration.

12.6.21

165

These flakes migrate slowly, evasively, from sky to ground.
Elegiac pilgrims, from heaven to earth. Pearl
Harbor Day. For me, the memory of a dark-eyed girl
who leapt from the Golden Gate. Salt waves resound

against the rocks, echo my fleet-footed cousin
sunk by violent destruction (50 years ago).
Each snowflake angles its own personal portfolio
of crystalline determination... (oh my Juliet Ravlin).

The Golden Gate fell, in Byzantium, on your birthday.
Each one's a personal specimen of human nature –
a Chosen One of the chosen ones. The Emperor
of oil & cream, of bread & wine. Of pine & jay.

If I find the warm wellspring of midwinter – the barn
where a child breathes in that homely scent of milk,
of beasts & straw... I will send you a note, snowflake.
Valentine of rose & seashell (straight from a sky-cairn).

12.7.21

166

In the depths, everything is *Law of the Sea*.
Tacit. Those lucent pearls are Jonah's eyes;
nothing of her ever dies; she is the life to be.
Her pigeon-scroll of seashell signals Paradise.

So Colossus of Rhodes becomes colossal rose

& Puritan severity conceals a kind of poetry.
John Winthrop, ravished in his dream
beneath his judge's robe of stern ferocity
felt the rose thread of Ariadne (*Notre Dame*).

12.8.21

167

Planed into piney Portland from Minneapolis,
like awakening to a moist dream-nest of green.
Like the Chinese Garden downtown – a meditation
of silence, sinuous dragon-water, peacefulness.

You were born in Providence, my son, my son
at *Women & Infants*, in late afternoon.
A first November snow was falling. Soon
your blue-eyed cries would still the highway din

outside that old Doyle Ave. tenement (for us,
anyway). & so yesterday (40 years later)
we walk & walk the river trail, while I labor
to gather our minds & hearts together. Jesus,

a little closer. Man is the *animale compagnevole*,
Dante claimed. & this is natural law : *the sense
of being right* (asserted glittering & fearless
Mandelstam). If only we could share the way!

His emblem was *goldfinch*. You are another bird.
Some kind of cautious, sharp-beaked, tentative
heron... wings wounded in the fight to live.
Old scars of unexpected blows – my broken word.

In *the pursuit of happiness*, our Janus-faced race
clusters in families & clans. In neighborhoods,
networks of commonalities. Our ebullient moods
of devoted exploration... tests of courage, grace,

disgrace. We walked in the rainy breeze, by railroad
tracks. Past a muted estuary (hawks gliding,

hunting, high overhead). A train went chugging
by, a little decorated Christmas train. You nod,

or shake your head... while I expatiate, & speculate
& reminisce. The wounds you don't understand
emit soft waves of suffering, from your azure &
disenchanted eyes. *The revolution will transmute all hate –*

this is your principle (you're not a *Shackmanite*,
you say). I don't believe it is the State,
myself – it's Roger's *LOVE*, that I had carefully forgot.
Refused to give. & so we trudge toward Advent night,

my son, my son.

12.14.21

168

A warm night in December. Tornado warning.
The tall northern pine at the prow of my house
grows old – a massive mast, shedding needles
smithereened by wind. Pregnant sails, whistling.

My father's lawbooks... great-grandfather's
Magna Carta (London, 1587). Selden Society's
blue tomes. The storm rescinds... *Thou ridest,
Lord.* Man is a butterfly. Even the worm is yours

to fling into the jet stream. Yet... now
an unpredicted calm descends. *Silent night.*
The flakes tack down, across Ireland... aslant
through Little Canada. Rime settles on each bow.

Each crystal almost equal to another, is almost
an *imago* of Thee. Light curtain for the darkness.
& this play of frozen teardrops... Hamlet's promise
paid? Fear not, Ophelia. Canonicus will be your host.

12.15.21

169

A grey December morning, brightened by snow.
A frisky breeze. The scene out my window –
Earth like a midshipman junco (flighty
charcoal salt). That northern spruce in majesty

by the front door. Ancient tree-presence, always
there... with an adolescent *arbor vitae* climbing
slowly beside it, almost hugging its trunk. & echoing
the outside, inside, this year's Christmas balsam. Rays

of its tiny lights twinkle, reflected in the glass.
The year floats along, slowly rotating on its axis,
like a coracle in some cosmic continuum. Your bliss,
Berkeley, dreaming of Bermuda there in Paradise,

Rhode Island; like that evergreen inventive mind
of Nicolas of Cusa, demonstrating how the joy
of intellectual freedom is the royal mark of the die.
Insignia of liberated human nature (God's, in kind).

The local is the locus; inimitable & irreplaceable.
Unique, distinct in place & time. *What already happened*
was the love you felt – like this fragrant pine stand
near Dante's Ravenna, or that Galilean crucible

of history (*Redemption* in the providential works).
Like that concord of grace & liberty & justice
which your mothers, fathers, labored to do justice –
promissory *Union*, woven covenant of singing larks.

The place was Providence; the man extraordinary Roger –
one bright mind & heart, forged in the legal kitchen

of Sir Edward Coke. His Narragansett refuge, hidden
with Canonicus – the kiln, the hearth-blaze (winter
          manger).

His anthropology, informed by cheerful fellow-feeling
(*animale compagnevole*, Whitman's *adhesiveness*)
foretold a world of magnanimity & lovingkindness;
his flinty & prophetic principle would bring

a new refreshment to the sense of human governance.
Political wisdom, high *Sophia* – rooted in a heart
that notes that wingèd, soaring innocence of spirit
kids incarnate (dreaming of plumcakes & peacefulness).

                    *

The bold straight line you drew between sacred
& secular, between divine & civic, between spirit
& flesh, was not a mark of separation, but
key signature for a consortium (maybe a Bach *prelude*)

of friendly instruments. Intrepid talents of good will
united by ineffable grace of Providence –
heart's natural *law of love*, reading the evidence
etched (by *blessed thirst for righteousness*) into the soil

of commonweal. Ebullient, inventive ghost of Nicolas
instill us with your magnanimous Renaissance
of understanding – lead us to your common sense
shared by meticulous spoon-maker, painstaking scholiast;

the *amassing harmony*, poured forth from galaxies
of glowing stars, effulgent billows of discovery;
that *higher law* of heavenly justice we descry

that filters down into our *Constitution* (all our argosies).

*

Nothing can efface the *Federal Triangle* of glory
& shame. The fate of Lincoln, JFK, & MLK...
measure of our national malice, & our misery.
Yet Emperor Justinian & Everyman Coke agree :

the natural law of righteousness is our palladium.

Isis, *Pallas Athena*... Sheba... most *Hagia Sophia*...
look down from your effulgent palisade of charity.
This emerald-violet *polis* we yearn to be
is trireme, *Pallada*, canoe... manger, *ecclesia*.

*

The power of the nations grinds through the slow days
like a clanking tank, like a meat-grinder. & its noise
cannot touch your soul, my child; its noise belies
your true compass, which points beyond this maze.

We are from below; Thou *art from above*. Time
& mortality cannot measure infinite fecundity;
when David danced before the covenantal Ark, he
stripped himself of all his royal robes (no crime

in Israel). We search to unfold your natural law,
Most High; we meditate upon it day & night;
your rightness filters down from such great height
even the North Star cannot trace your bear-paw,

YHWH. We are transfigured in a twinkling, at the end –

the only monarch is a butterfly. Archangel
Michael waves his wand... Satan returns to hell;
Oblomov's *Pallada's* on the doubloon's obverse. Send

to Petersburg to find the touchpiece in his mouth –
Joseph, Jonah; it will relieve both scrofula & scurvy,
sailorman. *Palladium helm* – ship of state, you see.
Out of the immemorial hive of *Union* (north & south)

equality emerges – out of Oneness, as its *Imago*.
Quadrivial unfolding (Thierry's blooming rose
window) is like a valentine, which Olga grows
in her Oblomov-dream of summer (*Ya vi lublyu*).

& the coin which Theseus finds in his labyrinth –
the obol Orpheus picks up, in Charon's boat –
that most minute, pervasive, copper mote...
a Lincoln penny, stamped in Ariadne's mossy mint.

The echo of the roar of nations follows the river
into its buried cave. The stars wheel slowly
far above... Bears, Twins, the Wain of Charlie;
the Earth turns slowly on its axis, furls its quiver

of oak-limbs – fleet coracle of coracles (the urn
of urns). A minuscule acorn stays hidden
in its canopy of rustling rough hands. Men
(Cavaliers & Roundheads) cannot find it. *Learn*

of the green world what can be thy place...
The green casque has outdone your elegance.
The restoration of the Earth... a seraph-glance
reveals it (as dawn light unfolds with natural grace).

But the smile of the seraph is a human smile.
& the *King of Kings* is an Everyman, an unknown
soldier climbing from his grave (ask Magdalen).
The restoration of your soul is your true trial –

your rood, your cross, your crossroad, Rhody Isle;
the only monarch is a butterfly; transfiguration
is her goal. She sails from Mexico to heaven
up the cedar's back, her vertical campanile –

her mast, her cross, her compass of the Law.
Nabokov, & Osip Mandelstam – Oblomov too
felt your royal almond bloom... your grail of yew
upon their lips. O starry union – fellowship of awe!

12.19.21

170

The night was bitter cold, Grandpa, on your birthday.
Saskatchewan was an Arctic Sea of snow.
That hulking concrete Peruvian flute, your granary
rose in the blue like a grave for a dead Pharaoh.

Your son, Uncle Jim, arrived just a month before.
He could never be President, I realized – born
as he was outside the 50 states. On a far shore
of the ocean, later on, he would combat imperial Japan

with all the rest. Pearl Harbor – that was his birthday.
The night was bitter cold, when his dismayed Juliet
wavered on a frozen rib of the Golden Gate. *Hey,
ey yo*. Will fathers ever weep? Have they ever yet?

The wars between the rival racketeers roll on.
They're lucrative. & treason is an opiate –
whatever you believe, bright thieves will reckon
gain. Quick flight, Mary... between Herod, Pilate.

1.6.22

171

We look for a poem like *Rose Island Lighthouse* –
useful for night pilots, lost in Narragansett Bay
or Newport yachters, gallivanting to Hyannis
or regular quahoggers, barefoot on the shore
who don't need directions, but simply love the light
like moths drawn to a lamp (over the surf's deep souse).

This week the International Society of Scientists
unfolded our Webb Telescope, up to its sunlit
gravitational equilibrium (*L2*). 18 hexagons
of ultra-thin beryillium, & gold. O such ornate
proportionate coordination! A rose, from thorns.
Humanity, O *compagnevole*! Your ultraviolet... *persists*.

& how many obsessive, miniaturist Maxwell Mays
can be compacted in a bird's-eye view of Providence?
Like Henry's sickly, glue-sniffed replica of *Constitution*
Rhode Island is the measure of a map so dense
it shrinks into a black-hole version of the nation.
What nation? America, America – your *End of Days*

Might be At Hand! Yet Nicholas of Cusa's semaphore
(theoretical pennant, flapping on the mast)
is a rude Renaissance mirror... RI idyll. Rigged
(by skippy *Ariadne*) to Connecticut. Conjectural, vast
& infinite (happy) benevolence, rooted in a rugged
enigmatic origami (of good will) – life's playful core.

The prairie woodland teemed with seekers of the light.
Earth itself was mother-world of sociable affection.
All the unwritten histories of human magnetism –
a witty congress of adhesiveness, laughter's secession

from the rote idolatry of each compelled iconoclasm.
Thy law, instilled within each heart : *the sense of being
    right.*

Meanwhile, across Fontanka bridge scurries... a mouse.
Oblomov, aboard the *Pallada*, imagines Hagia Sophia
with a million milky eyes of human wisdom – Russian
motherland, Ethiopian Sheba-land... some Beulah-
Paradise. George Berkeley's chaste & puddingstone
sea-rose. *Eternity*, O *Eternity*! – *that is our business*.

172

I see you barreling down a sand-bare isle, in Paradise –
cartwheeling artlessly (toward Skye vanishing point)
like a Canonicus 4-leaf clover, held in a Henry vise.
Your face, only his canoe construction? *Anoint*

me, sweetly nimble one, with your enfolding, absolute

trust. Love-deeded arrowhead... Ariadne Sophie-thread...
Come, come, haunted dune-kin – *piccola Farfalla*!
Unspool, babbling yo-yo, from Luck to Shakespeare's
            Head
(in Providence); hold near my heart, rose beryl-eye.

2.11.22

173

Truth shines in the distance, like Hagia Sophia
by the Golden Horn. & the distance is a measure
of your probable deflection, from its pure splendor –
the simple freedom of brave innocence (a *Fontegaia*
fountain, bubbling with infant glee). Yet this foggy lens
is fractured *Imago* – your smiling enigma, making amends.

My Providence is merely a mumbled commonwealth.
Your mind's invention, when the heart stirs, slightly
(barely). A single petal on a burial rose (stealthy
death only a drowsy sleep). Good will, beyond wrath.

& if I lived there once, & carved a fatal track
you lived there too, at least as just as well –
on that island road, beside the sea-flecked shore,
under a turquoise porch, atop a moss-green shack;
it was your Blackstone oak; it was your gall that bore
the honey-hive of heart, the surging wave's sea-bell.

1.12.22

174

Winter daylight through an eastern window
lingers tenderly on the old Christmas trinkets,
children's baubles on the sill. A wooden
3 Wise Men – grown thin, straight, straightened; one
retractable *Nutcracker* king; a clay *King David*, brow

molded to solemn wonder now (watching eternity).
Old men in winter season grow lenticular – they
fast so slowly, down to plain transparent stone.
Hands roughen like archaic deeds of property –
scars of Canonicus & Miantonomi (*arrow*, *canoe*).

Four centuries of sea air in the Ocean State
soften the documentary parchment like old hands.
The light grows tender as their touch. An absolute
trust. King Duncan faced Macbeth with such a faith
his fate belied – or rather sealed in blood (Scotland's).

An old man turns toward the center, like a spinning
pine-top, losing momentum. Your *word*, an agate
gate. Your *stone*, a coppery grail (from Camelot,
or Newport). & your *life*, a welcome feast – brimming
with rectitude & joy (loving *equality*, becoming one).

1.13.22

175

The sea, the sea, the Ocean State. It is
the beforehand, signalling through everything –
firmly, timed with your heart. & that rose
will sing – mauve, violet, meek; folding, enfolding.

So the red white & blue, at their lonely Waterloo
fuse through their scars (copper penny, bronze
star). Unto this sea-oracle, manifest for you –
its prow an origami beryl-crown (translucent *Pax*).

Through your cloud-river thunderhead of stars
through your infinitude of restless creatures
the mute rightness of your *sea-law* mirrors
the beam of each dark lighthouse – mine, yours.

So thy veteran bread was cast upon the water.
So the mild martyrs for soft *orthos logos*
lift at dawn, along the shore, their sweet sea-rose –
a Jubilee-reunion hearth; *tout-monde* Sophia's laughter.

1.15.22

176

Still sunlight, at the nadir of a frozen arc.
A history of snowfall (over the *Masonic Center
of Brain Science*). What lights the human spark
across these blankety wastelands of space? Her
flinty look. One tiny flicker of his hand. *Sail Boat*,
by Marsden Hartley (1916) – flesh-tone panes
of canvas, stretched into an air of sea. One note
wrung from a prairie void... a flight of cranes.

8 Bells. *A Friend Against the Wind* (blue plume
floating rightward, from a golden Easter crossbun
cup). *Adelard the Drowned, Master of the Phantom*
(rugged sailor, bearded, pelted – pink carnation
lighting like a sparrow on his ear). The Perfect
is the Good made flesh, made suffering thing.
A smiling Black man, walking toward his intersect,
his hour – carrying a scroll made honey. Sink to sing.

*

The Law of Nations does not apply at sea. There
be a feud state between states everywhere.
Unnatural interest trumps irenic lore
& righteousness is servant to *realpolitik*.
We must uphold ill-usage to the end, sick
as we are – Glory is Pride, & Love is War!
So every rising notion bakes its Janus-face :
our good is absolutely good – especially for us.

Whales swim in the ocean. Jonah's in the whale.
They marvel together at the multiprocity of life –
how spools of Medusa unite all things in grief,

love. Nothing's itself (only a human mirror-shell).

O Felix Culpa! Last name's actually O'Toole.
Guy's a mick lives off Little Crow (So. St. Paul).
Stashed loot (gravelly, some say) in Minneapolis;
black MLK money, Twin Cities coinage, counterfeit.
Drove Thunderbird – all knew was gonna get it
gilded, eventually. Woe-man, come dimly into focus.
Link to sacrifice... twin beds? On your conscience,
Jonasgamos. Naked at the equality dream (U-Ninevents).

*

You, my beloved, are a plurality of yourself,
the Lady sighed – like a rent in the fabric,
like a brick in the current, like a canned-heat
elf, a leper in the goatscape... where opposites
meet. I loved it when she sang that, Frederick –
Manfred, maid of my heart'sblood! A figure *8*
she was, lounging in my spectacles... stood up
iffinighty straight, & walked – the Continental Shelf!
As if out o'the sea came – Shelley A. Keats, to sup!
As if out o'the earth came Jeanne of Anchorage,
wi' precious Cup! So Clover wheeled her cartilage,
to rage no more – a smiley infant, playful pup,
born to prink atop them gurgling gargoyles
disconcerting Chartres, she was (as Henry gnawed).
'Twas not the nothing then but human, pine
to vine – a gap aglow in Ariadne-tread, O'Ryan.

*

The baleful eye of social hatred turns this way & that
like a vain wind, shifting atop its iron resentment pole.

232

But your warm whisper seeps from tacit well. To heal.
The milk & honey of familial grace (your father's hat,

you mother's hug). Ambrogio Lorenzetti's *Allegory*

of Good Government – regal *Justitia*, Empress of God;
calm lovely *Pax*, at rest upon her pillowed couch
in summertime. Sheep follow blind, by touch.
Up starry trails... seeking good grass, abjuring bad.

*

The arc of the moral universe is long
but it bends toward your lips, O high & holy
Sophie. *The greatest force in the universe is love.*
& history is not a nothing Mars, nor the lonely
surliness of inhuman imagination – it is a strong
man, shackled, behind bars. Give him a shove
toward freedom, if you can. Walk apart
with him, a little while; listen to your heart.
Once upon a time, upon a bright spring day
in Providence, I looked out the library window,
& there, with cane, limped Bishop Desmond Tutu –
smiling, laughing, doing a little dance (his way)
down Power Street. *Behold, my strength*
in weakness is perfected. & so the thread
of Ariadne stretches, catenary, all its length
along an arc of mercy. Risen from the dead.

*

The Ark is long, O, the arc is long. A
streaming continuum of light-years. Unaccountable
quanta of cubit-spans. I think the essential

woe-man is a long-term jobber – Ariadne
writing her Webb-telescopic thesis... Odysseus
sharing odd matrimonial intuitions, with Penelope
(*prodigal, probably come home someday*). Meekness
is living with such sailor ignorance (blind otherness).

Until He comes to tear down Kings & Powers...
Roger, in London, with his friend Milton. *A key
to open a box of keys.* Twin stars of prophecy –
like this bronze escutcheon : caskets of emperors
& pharaohs echoing, heraldic, over one mudlark
doorhinge (pulled from the Thames). A little room
with a single gate... a ray of light through the dark.
A thread tugs your soul (piloting *Ocean River* gloom).

Breath of air betwixt you & me, between *I & Thou*.
A pregnant pause, a silence in the universe.
It was freedom, of course, at root of thy *kenosis*,
Lord. Double-humbling O, kind servant, at the prow.

*

Just zero degrees today. A farthing, far in height.
Across from the *Brain Science Center*, in the dead
of winter (intermittent tocsin of the heart).
I seek to enunciate your *Word*. Crane for what's unsaid.
My penny is a muddy dented coin, off in the distance
& my ark is wobbling athwart her own long wake
& yet your Union is not fractured by my dissonance,
nor is Love's equilibrium undone – it cannot break.

Heart flickers, hums so, slightly. Muted snare.
Adam & Eve, learning to bear each other. Bending
like boughs, in mutual renunciation – to share,

give, love. Jonah's *kenosis*, after almost drowning,
weaves a mournful stricken Nineveh (of give & take).
The push of man's aggression, all his troubled sleep –
cast of a horseshoe, mold of rusty stone. *O Mandrake*!
Icon of Medusa! *Mayapple of Maximus*! Rise from the
     deep.

1.18-26.22

177

We had a melting day today, in Minneapolis.
For a little while, anyway. Phantom of spring.
I am beset by haphazard memory... & this
might be a good thing. I remember well-being,

wells of well-being. A little tree on Sycamore St.
in Providence, one sultry August summer night.
Abstractions, full of Narragansett sand. Sweet
rancid sea of actuality (almond-brown eyes, demure,

smolder with tempered flame). We see what we can,
& wait for common sense to smooth the cracks –
like absent-minded, smiling Justice Breyer, his élan
for civilization (life more affectionate than all our hacks

& querulous quacks would have). Ideology might be
your personal rabbit's-foot of faith, but reason
is a plain highway, mild weather to eternity;
Love's fairest knot of reciprocity is justice done

(by rule of human dignity). Little Rhody is my own
inchoate, incomprehensible rose apse of rhapsody –
canonical birchbark lens (Canonicus & Miantonomi)
for lifting safely up Roger, from waves of snow & poison...

& although you might be from Kansas or Poughkeepsie,
or St. Pete or Paul, or Istanbul, the human mind
is complete palladium – ruby or beryl, raw, refined –
a cave, designed so *concavex*, that we can only see

what we feel, feel what we see (like Pinetop Perkins,
Eyesight to the Blind). This way to the exit

is the other way, & Maximus & his dry biscuit
radiate light beams, like murmurs from the Bosporus

& in this darkened mirror every human soul
embarks for Trebizond, without an ounce of gold
& every heart trembles, & every wolf will howl
at the gibbous moon, like a scimitar – like a *dhou*

off the mole outside Newport (near Paradise).
& I remember now another August moon, riding
calm, huge & silent off the Narragansett quays.
Your tides, lifting the Earth by gentle force – only

a sigh, sign of your breaking shore, my broken heart;
only a mirror, a curving spinnaker – tossed by wind
across a glittering sea... a sea of galaxies... a tiny part
of one cosmos (which only tides of *Agape* can bind).

& as George Berkeley (on his puddingstone cave-throne,
in Paradise) sensed the intellectual splendor of his dream-
creation – so you'll intuit, apprehend this Rhody-zone
of moonlit Providence; just as blind, battered Milton

thought back to those barren winter mornings in London,
when he & voluble Roger Williams gathered firewood
for the pale sputtering hearthsides of the poor (one
Conscience stirs the embers of each conscience, dude).

So light seeps deeper into every local instance, every
instant. So Justice Breyer's gentle common sense
is of that *higher law*, which reigns o'er land & sea –
AMOR beyond each marble-roam (sails, mobile tents).

*

237

These black winter branches have a late Brahms look
beneath their frail, cloud-filtered sun. Yet you are
always there – already waiting for me, *Mystère.*
Your heart sheds leaves, from the most ancient book.

O Shipwright of a million-eyed Argo, *lifting your rood*

The silence of a simple one is hers, is yours. Is here.
Comes to restore you, to yourself. The king
of sheep is but a shepherd, feeding, bearing, piloting;
his human law is everlasting. Listen, Rose; draw near.

*

The far-off February sun slightly cheers the air
floating frigid over the vast snow blanket. Like
a planetary spinnaker, set for an Earth locked
stubbornly in ice, dockside. Heavy snow, over there

too (in Providence). & dense indeed is little Rhody,
in my mind – like that intense dark summer green
spread out below the bird's-eye, post-colonial scene
flickered (so subtly) by Maxwell Mays. It must be

the steeple of First Baptist, then – tall wooden axle
at the center of his oil-slick swirl – a denominational
spin-off, one of Roger's ventures (experimental,
temporal) grown so large now – maximous, maximal...

Such an anti-gravitational thrust in those brush-strokes!
Roger Williams, pushing his canoe across the choppy Bay
like a dauntless Maori Odysseus... guiding his party
of Polynesian aquanauts into glittering sky-spokes

of an immaculate, midnight Pacific. O the fortitude,
the intrepid onwardness of the human race!
Flinging Ariadne's microscopic threads out into space
to unpack origami lids of a Webb-telescope, & brood

upon the cosmic fireplace... gaze into remotest
origins! Relentless march of technological progress!
Humaniac drive – cracking wide open every riddling
          recess!
Why then do I peer so into this dark backyard... the past?

The yard there, at 132 6th. A summer night
over a tiny forest-green farmhouse. Sound
of music... resonant bass-line, beneath the wound
of Odetta's trembling wing. *One Grain of Sand*. Right.

There's a knot in the heart which is harder... denser...
more massive than spacetime. Where the impulse
to love & hate meets the swelling crowd (indifference,
incipient chaos). Where *One* becomes *Many* – the
          answer,

the question. Why *the King Must Die*?
Why love must end? Why the world revolves
around a musty movie theater? Where a song solves
nothing... just a yearning memory. In your eye,

little Rhody (at the *Avon Cinema*). O foursquare
character of Roger, on his hilltop – courage,
magnanimity, kindness... giving to this little village
a global, cosmic, comic relevance. It's in the air,

Squire... it's in the shire. & it was always there.

239

Canonicus knew it – Miantonomi too. *Orthos
logos*... the rightness of the universe. Jesus
was smiling when he tuned his parables... mirror

for a new, kind humankind. We are taking Earth
on a canoe-trip, friends – to the Big Bang
Archipelago, to the Golden Gate; when *morning
stars sang all together*, & *Argo* rowed into her berth.

& the massive rose, that simmers in your heart
like the core of a planet, like a world in pain...
she skips like Silky, twirls an emerald once again;
crown on her head, she's *compagnevole* (wheeling her
        cart).

                            2.1.22

178

The news that Monica Vitti (regal one) has died
arrives on this stark-frozen February day.
Her obituary quotes the riddle she replied
when asked about the missing heroine in *L'Avventura* :

remember, when last we see her, she holds two books –
the Bible, and *Scott Fitzgerald's* Tender is the Night.
& in that novel too, the protagonist mysteriously books
almost before the book begins. Tender is the night,

indeed. Far below zero. I think of Mandelstam
in Vladivostok, before he disappeared; I imagine
even at the end, he cheered with his stamina the jam
of suffering prisoners. The poet's spirit is stubborn.

It's not so much *nostalgia for world culture*, but the grip
of a climber hanging from a cliff – his apprehension
of a vast serene expansive plenitude, as on a ship
the topmast lookout rides a crest of the Pacific Ocean –

smooth curving speeding effortless & lovely glide
until that *oceanic feeling* of the whole wide universe
is yours, as well. Is every infant's deepest need –
is every child's birthright – despite the curse

of bodily mortality (which shall be overcome, also).
What else could poetry be for? We remember
in our bones, that blessed & ineradicable unison
of all with all – integrity of Thierry's high number

One; our breathing conscience yearns continuously
to berth itself once more in that sweet motherland

vessel – almond tug of Ilya's Olga, piloting Mary's
heart-shaped *Pallada* (his valentine from Trebizond).

Thus when I turn back in my mind's eye to Rhode Island
these rose-tinted glasses sparkle with those actual sea-
roses : there again, rocked by Newport waves, on sand
like JFK, half-sleeping with his open book (*Great Gatsby*?

maybe *Journey to the Center of the Earth*) aboard
his baby sailboat, with its oscillating mast (waving,
waving, back & forth, to shore). Imagining, *begorrah*,
that bug-gored bog turned Roger-*Gorod*. Saving

the best wine for last. Bringing that rigorous
fellowship of Williams to the all-human table
of good will – a massive mass of gleeful, riotous
civility – the *Bog-Goret*, the *akme* of the fable –

steaming kitchen of affectionate *domestic hellenism*
so hebraic in its heartfelt righteousness, that
Tsvetaeva & Akhmatova, Gumilev & Mandelstam
fluted, fifed & fiddled all through that Soviet night

until, finally, we got the message, & began to dance
as well, as Will, as one... around a shapely *Grail* –
around that seaborne memory, dissolving distance
& restoring every mossy rusted anchor, without fail;

that *Ocean State*, where once upon a time
a beloved woman disappeared beneath the wave
of time itself, & of indifference – that *felix* crime
that brings us to our senses... out of the grave.

*

Thermometers inch just above zero. It is
indeed a darkish coldish day. Silly expatriates
expatiate, expansively, toward cosmopolitan delight –
vast *Ocean State*. A little room remains, full of remorse.

Your crossweft, sea-borne gift, Penelope... calm unicorn.

Down from Summit heights, on top of the Dome
a golden *Independent Man* lifts up his lance. Yet
salt is in the wind. We are far from home. Only
your agate lamp, sweet *Liberty*, our freedom grants.

                              *

The desolation in *Deserto Rosso*, amid the bright
primary colors slapped on steel bulkheads
outside Ravenna; the delicate pathos, the slight
breeze of stoic humor Monica (in moss-green) sheds

wandering among those docks & sheds. The *beautiful
people* – who have learned to cope, function &
engineer, but forgotten how to love. Remote sun
through autumn haze, across the marshlands. The tall

yellow giraffes of telephone cranes. & that aged
eccentric painter, with his mule-cart of gray
paint-cans, who's painted himself into an alley
cul-de-sac (Antonioni, maybe – maestro *photo-negativa*,

run ragged). Sorrow at heart. A bleak despair
of unloved loveliness. The Existentialist believes
in man's nobility – expressed in action everywhere
against the Nothingness. The Anthropologist conceives

243

post-humanism – reality is but a cybernetic system
of differentials working themselves out against
a blank background of artificial noise. Me? I'm
an Incarnationalist. There is a Marsden benevolence

takes multifarious forms... forms like our own
on Earth. Like those immense and silent icons
in shadowy vaults of *Sant'Apollinare*. Where
Monica would go (to lean her head on stones).

I once won a quiz contest for the RI Historical Society.
The prize was a little square tabletop stone coaster
imprinted with Roger Williams' compass (remarkably
still ruggedly intact, in the archive). He was a *Seeker*,

so he said. Of mental cast, Baconian (unmystical,
empirical). Thus to be human is to seek the *Orient* –
Pole Star, magnetic North (even without a paddle,
if need be). *I am nothing without your circling tent*

of galaxies, *Wakan Tanka* (whispered his great friend,
Canonicus). Edgar Poe, in Brady's photograph
in the Atheneum. A man in despair – man at the end
of his psychic subway. Only a reeling, wandering epitaph

without Helen (Whitman... just down the street).
Crane, quoting Blake – *right thro' the Gates of Wrath*
humanity must go : to find the solace of complete
experience – to win the glory of each life-in-death.

A winter sun sets now, through burnt-out Notre Dame.
In camp near Vladivostok, shuddering Mandelstam
intones a silly, reedy song – for a spark of fellowship

among the living dead. When the *Nazir* came

reciting into Nazareth, hefting his lumber tools
he shed a hopeful sound – something he'd learned
from his father's smoky scent, his mother's curls –
their smiles, their voices. O flowering almond,

you are already here, almost. The vernal season,
the blooming days, are still ahead, the month
of melting ice & valentines is with us now. *Heaven
is integral; flowers are immortal* – O my sturdy terebinth.

2.3-5.22

179

February. Lunar New Year for East Asia –
first rumor of spring in the air. At Orchestra
Hall, young Chinese women dance the orange
paper lantern dance, miming the plangent

Obon ceremony (of Japan). & I remember
those blazing-orange Japanese-lanterns, popping up
in the backyard – each with an edible red berry-drop
hidden inside, like tiny dangling piñata prize. Sure!

In Providence, on Fisher St. – when life was sweet.
Through my rose-tinted Rhody glasses, it seems
we were like sand pebbles aboard the *San Pablo*.
We were *one grain of sand, one drop of water*

in the deep blue sea... Odetta crooning on the radio.
When Jake Holman was a holm oak, one whole man
rather than black hole – vast jakes, a-swirling O
for grouting off the waste of all our violence & sin...

– & so ol' Henry patch together him *Giuseppe*-coat.
Him kind of RI-edification scheme – like that
old coot in Ravenna, the old man of *Ms. Placet
Wi-Ping Concrèt-Ness*, in moss-green wool jacket

limping into your empty, cavernous *cattedrale*
(her only constant, borrowed from Constantinople –
& cordial Emperor Justinian, just beyond the pale
would brim with almond joy to know). *Vale,*

valley of ash & bones. We will remember you.
These ghosts of Buchenwald & Hiroshima

fold into frozen tears of snow – the deep bayou
of our amnesia (*one star*... colder than Antarctica).

The inventive bickering of the intellectuals
is rather artistic, each in its own way. Dissonance
is newness. Opens the equal temperament of wells –
submerged tones tucked behind each cock's prance

of *maestro Compositore*. Si. So Giotto will out-jot
Piero della Francesca... or was the other way around?
Can't recall. I remember *Madonna della Parto* –
snow meandering (outside *Women & Infants*) down

to ground. I remember how my blind
self-serving *libertine mores* destroyed our love –
O arrogance of young men (psychic bind
of narcissism). Yet *caritas* comes from above...

agape, slanting down like snow. An equilibrium
of desolation – truth like salt, like winter stars
swirled in the frozen barrel (Mandelstam).
Equality is justice, thus. Just this (beyond the wars).

Fold me an origami heart, Sophie... fold me
a paper memory. Fold me a rose-colored almond
mandorla – fold me a Penny Williams piano
melody. Fold me a hat to sport, to that *tout-monde*

Restoration festival – make me an acorn coracle
to stay afloat, across your cosmic *Ocean State*.
Love is the *Argo* keel, our only holm-oak oracle –
one Arctic blue-eyed woman in Firenze (checkmate).

*

As a child, I built bridges with string (thin
catenary smiles); *Constitutions* with Elmer's Glue.
I played piano at MacPhail – *Autumn Leaves*, version
by Roger Williams – hands shaking like leaves. (True.)

Your mother's parchment fingers sketched a world once,
    too.

We fold our hearts (like origami) into everything we do.
Oblomov spent his obol at the Styx (his personal Obon
ceremony, Olga). Joachim Fiore, in his cavern, drew
a plummeting eagle. Dove's rescue – Jonah's restoration.

                          *

On your *Night Sea*, Agnes, the thin gold glimmers
in a frame, in a grid. A constellation (across
remote night blue). I think of Verrazzano's cruise
round Narragansett Bay (in 1524); an albatross

skims through the dark, a shadow just above the mast.
& high beyond, the *Bears*, the *Wain*, the *7 Sisters*
twirl a slow & stately sarabande (around Polaris).
One triangular-shaped island, like Rhodes, he murmurs

into his notebook – echoed for centuries to come
(& new seekers). The steadfast stars, the sturdy
mast. Not long before, Gioacchino da Fiore (plumb
for prophecy) foretold *the Aeon of the Spirit.* She

would plummet like a rainbow eagle, he sketched out –
spread feathers like a dove-cloud, into the hearts
of humankind (on Earth). Like *Thunderbird* (shout

loud, children!) – a bolt of fire, fusing all quartets

to one *communitas*. Lent is coming, kids. After
Mardi Gras. We'll eat biconvex lentils, only –
polish lenses for the night voyage (that rafter-
life beckons me, mate). We'll cross the high sea

of *Ocean River*. Last year, in January, they
besieged the Federal Triangle – assaulted *Lady Liberty*
with every stratagem of fraud, & vicious perfidy.
I thought about the ghosts of Abraham, & JFK,

& MLK – watching, watching yet (from their dark
high *otherworld*, beyond this clay). I don't know what
to say. Whatever I may babble misses the mark.
Heart's high *agape* – love's *eucharist* – is secret

from these sad, mad dogs of war. Yet they are brothers,
sisters... my fellow Americans. It is a riddle
worthy of the Greek tragedians. & yet the answer's
easy, in a way. *Seek justice*, beyond all this fiddle –

beyond our scramble for pelf & glory (all this
red-blue, bruised-plum vanity). & *what is justice*?
Ask that Seeker on the hill – Roger, magnanimous.
It is your warm adhesive fellowship – the love-embrace

of one whole human race; it is that *higher, natural
Law*. Of equal men & women, everywhere.
Around the globe, across the universe... our special
Kingdom of the lion, & the lamb – our *Ocean* atmosphere.

& I remember walking into downtown Providence
with Penny Williams, daughter of the slaves

249

of these Plantations. I remember gathering evidence
to bring to City Hall... that justice every seeker craves.

& I remember Ellen Ryan, daughter of a Bridgeport
cop – from Holy Cross, to VISTA volunteer, to light
like that *Rose Island Light*. Shining from Federal Court
to Washington – lifted to dignity (of every human right).

& I remember Mary Negus too (my mother's mother);
child of Quaker farm, in West Branch, Iowa –
painting her scene, like Maxwell Mays. Calm seeker
after equilibrium... that steeple stinging like a bee
          (*alleluiah*).

2.7-8.22

180

You too were that lunatic lover once, in Rhode Island –
when a massive moon hovered low over the Bay
like an opalescent coracle; when I heard your voice
murmur back to me, like Narragansett surf – calm &
relaxed; drowsy, peaceful. As if an unknown law was
leading the way, & this *Old Man of Misplaced
            Concreteness*
flecked his gray waves beneath her mauve chalk valentine.

Your origami collage contains so many classroom faces,
Sophie. So does mine. There's Penny, there's William –
two copper coins, spelling *meek liberty*; there's traces
of Sally, & Ellen, & mordant Penelope... (Jenny's a clam).

WPA Roger, levitating off his cliff, was lunatic, too –
the vista of the *VISTA* volunteers was his as well.
There is a *common good* in the *pursuit of happiness*,
if only we will. This copper serpent is our ruddy coign;
this wisdom, innocent as Jonah's mourning shells. *Who*,
who, calls Pallas, from her   palace; *You-who*, keens
            Ishmael,
from his wishing-well. Ineffable cloud-sigh. Witness.

2.14.22

181

In sickness, in the dead of winter, you hear things
seldom heard clearly. The flat sound of a train horn
between flat stretches of gray cloud, white snow. Pings
of triangular backyard birds, harping on winter corn.

My father, glimpsed for a moment through the filter
of a sun-bleached awning (in a Scott Fitzgerald book).
His serious social awkwardness. Me, the drifter
with sophisticated style, tossing sticks into a brook

of Styx. The earth is heavy, plain & cold
this time of year. We flit around, collecting ideas
of corn – like small grain elevators. *To have, to hold.*
Grace is not what we reach for (that would be weakness).

Your woodpecker sports a racy crimson stripe.
Like a crystal spearhead through a golden crown.
Our fumbling efforts at self-government... only a type
of primeval promise. Shekinah's hayfield (new-mown).

2.16.22

182

Just as a tiny drop of India ink
suffuses the whole sky in an ocean of blue,
I wish your russet splinter of the past
might color the future with its early hue
of crimson rose. & I am just a figment
of remote reunion. A loafing, desiccated crust
of other seasons, other seas. *Sponge, drink.*

One infinitesimal spearpoint of poison
tempers our present & presents our cure.
One snowflake of galactic gravitation
lifts each trundling planet in its mirror.

One springtime half a century ago
a child with a fever, lying by the windowsill
listened to the ordinary sounds outside –
kids' glee, train-honks, bird-chatter's trill.
Each note a tone fragment of a fundamental
tide-chorale, a bobbing bottle on an ocean ride;
small portent of a Jubilee. Rose scent you know.

2.18.22

183

Is it real, then? Can your little Rhody be
a *key that opens a box of keys*? Can a 13th state
be an *Ocean State*? & is the Messiah in Galilee?
If only Nicholas were here, to help me contemplate.

Or George, with his lenticular cloud-canoe (in Paradise).

But we only see what we do. We have to.
If I open my heart, I see the shame of callous shells.
Indifference, dishonesty, remorse... & your violet, too.
Sprung from rose-quartz granite – April's tide-wells.

2.19.22

184

The poem scrapes like a wave across a pebble beach.
It is dumb. It is mute. It is a sense. It is a sense
of touch. Back, forth. & the spine of each wave
is the urge of the sea. So it is, near Providence.
I felt the brick-dust poverty of absent factories,
where VISTA kids from Holy Cross encamped (to save
transactional America from her own splinter-speech).

My own muteness flows into Narragansett Bay.
My quartz isle clings like a barnacle to Massachusetts
& Connecticut – what makes a granite dream I cannot say.
It's there, like almond in an eyelid; Thierry at Chartres.

& I see Roger, in New England winter, with his arms
flung wide toward Canonicus, & all his tribe, who open
theirs as well. I see them smile. I hear them laugh.
Thierry reaches back through azure, toward the One –
beata Marie, beaming down from Ocean. *The mind
        measures*!
Cusanus cries. Divine justice, & human law – one graph
matrix, one common life. One crown of quahog charms.

2.21.22

185

That old man of crumbling concrete, tilting up there
over the cliff, must find his center of gravity
before long. His middle C, or 44th key –
as you, Penelope, have been for me. A spiral stair

leading into a refectory – where Piero della Francesca
limned his *Madonna*, centered on her own dark almond
(burgeoning toward spring). We were young & fond
when you deployed your catenary thread (*selah*)

like a threnody of gravity, between two iron nails
or like the shadow of a smile, beneath a sundial.
& so that old man's stone heart moves. Meanwhile
a featherweight vista of Maxwell Mays exhales,

& we recall – *we are but mingling, gamboling players
here on Prosper's bent, lopsided isle.* I am nothing
but a stone statue, without you. & we who sing
Hagia Sophia, & our almond joy... (forgive these airs).

2.22.22

186

The knots you wove into your schoolgirl unicorn
resting now in Susan's stairwell on Savoy (across
from Redeemer) are parts of one whole & weighty
rose-quartz element. Like the arc of a coin-toss
twirling on a continuum, from *Sheep's Clothing*
to *132 6th* (all around Providence). A mighty
tiny conjunction, Ariadne : threads of being born.

The poem – icon, simple semblance of communion –
spins an analogy, the way my *Constitution* replicates
the simple oneness of a natural law : we are all human.
&, as such, we mimic someone ghostly... *Hail, shipmates.*

& perhaps we are Hagia Sophia, *with a million eyes...*
& perhaps your rapture is a universal rhapsody.
For human dignity can never be repealed, your lips
keep mumbling; it can only be restored. Like the bee-
hive in the oak tree, your deep hum makes the keel sing,
Penelope – the thrum of your frame booms agate-skips
across the Black Sea, back to me. Your almond never dies.

2.23.22

PART FOUR

187

A sea-breeze off the harbor at Kherson
braces the canvas – lines creak against the mast.
Old yearning to set sail, at dawn.
I was a galley slave at the Pancake House
for a while, in Providence. I threw all my LPs
in the dumpster on my way out of town. I was light,

back then. I was 3/5ths of a man, for a while.
Good & evil played chess for my soul –
Stalin, stolen Anna (Florence)... you know the rest.
The wheel spins... Hamlet's life ain't worth a mouse
(*Ophelia, Ophelia*) since Denmark spilled the beans
for Norway – *bloody, treasonous, cursèd spite.*

Why do the nations rage? Does the ghost shake foils?
A shivering hare waits in Dürer snow, to be done
with war. Don't mind these boils –
I'll be dead before dawn. *We shall embark at last
on the* Last Day, *children* (take the train, dear spouse).
The list is deep, the sea's blue-black. We'll set it right.

3.5.22

188

It is not holy but infernal fire
rains down on these cathedrals in Ukraine.
Dreams of one gray-suited rodent of dominion;
delusions of a lost, ambitious bureaucrat
from Hell. *Yet we have beheld the humble empire
of your law*, YHWH – *sweet* agape *is all that you require.*

After the storm, *en voyage* from Byzantium
I see his bright glance, the seraph-smile
of Nicholas von Kues. Earth is Man's imperium – yet
God's immeasurable benevolence rebukes our guile.

Meanwhile, that baby-faced comedian from Kyiv
molts, inconceivably, to prince of peace.
Minotaur, bent human image of the beast
resents the graceful spires, would lay them flat –
such emperors can never give, only receive. Yet
still our dove (Jonah the Ark) murmurs... *love*, *live*.

3.7.22

189

Today Beckmann's *Departure* swam into my mind's eye.
The cabaret travesty of sadistic persecution twists
its Dantesque perversion of love into a barbed-
wire cage on either side; & yet, afloat at the center,
the Queen, the Child, the King, the Prince set sail –
away from evil's emptiness, into *pleroma*-realm of blue.

So let's imagine the common good as a cosmic ocean.
Behold these awkward, hulking, heroic human figures,
like glowing mirrors in whorled galaxies of bird-nests.
Imagine the oneness of perennial happiness, as if you
lived in a wave-curved corner of Hagia Sophia – your joy
one sigh of compassionate wisdom (like Valentine in jail).

The benchmark is there. It was always there,
like a wooden frame around your epileptic tarantella –
a *pianissimo* finger-step, tracing your daubed dolphin-
prow (your figurehead of *Liberty*). A lighthouse, garbed
in origami mirror-folds – Rose Island... *Promised Land...*
beside you, your unfailing friend (your Lenten harbinger).

3.8.22

190

The strongmen take by force what they can justify
neither by reason or persuasion. My dear Irma,
they are but thieves – they cannot look you in the eye.
Calm waves erase their scrolls of sand (amen, *selah*).

The air's too still. A cypress warns with one cicada.

For every hollow syllable, someone will pay.
For each blood-rusted coin, someone must die.
The Earth is washed in stringent salt. Even today
cold shadows fall from clouds, make children cry.

3.8.22

191

Every millimeter of the cornered circle must uphold
your limpid dome beside the sea. & this microcosm
(like Leonardo's *Vitruvian Man*) will be your compass,
little Henry, when you go teeter-totter... like Berryman
over the abyss, or like Roger Williams (blind inchworm
at the mercy of a Narragansett storm) edging
(shaky hand outstretched) along his cliffside plank.

& if, like Hamlet on board ship, I cry havoc
amid these rasping, slippery dogs of war – *who then
will hear me*? & so I furl my furry costume, prepping
the be-mirrored revelation of Rose Island Lighthouse –
whose ghostly deacon is a kind of brooding eminence
himself... stone shepherd, starting to move... (his fold).

The smallest things are often the strongest things, Hen.
Give your conscience liberty, *my child*, counsels the Block
Island iconoclast (*My People Is the Enemy*). Because
life most of the time is a mode of *fill in the blank*
doesn't mean you can't look up to blue sky (now
& then) – or the clear impeccable stars. *Amen*, Ocean.

3.10.22

192

The circle of ash at the center of her shining brow
& the bitter herbs at the breaking of the fast
remind us how that extra chair for Elijah, Henry
at the center of the rippling, unfolding Rose
is not an ego-trip for you – among blind Adams
you may be most blind. *My filmy lamps are squinty, dim.*

& even with the flinty compass of Roger Williams
that circle whose center is nowhere & circumference
everywhere remains ineffable, as grace of Boethius –
& raying from each rosy heart... our Kinneret becalms.

Still, on my rusty American map, Little Rhody remains
a tiny, salted rudder for the nation. & as the prow
of my heart, stringfelled, turns toward Penelope
her Ariadne-thread glistens... grows taut... *thrums* –
her Achaean acacia-keel unveils its arcing dolphin-glose :
the law of the sea is an Ocean State; *Jonah emerges at the
        last.*

3.11.22

193

On the screen you saw the snow cling to the roads
& the cratered houses. Where they left their keys
on the crippled bridge, when they tried to flee
with their blood-spattered suitcase. The snow was
buffeted by a bright March wind, that none can see –
it turned away this family, before they could leave.

& weaponry kept falling. & if there is *a key*
that opens a box of keys, as my exile proclaimed
it must be in the key of *aye*, and in the key of *oh*
it must be the key into the babbling of everybody –
it must be the blood we share (the strong, the maimed).

Prokofiev, for example, transposed all the white keys
out of *Peter & the Wolf* – from the key of C
into another string, near Voronezh. It was 1935,
I think; it was near the end of the score (*Leaves*
of Autumn) Roger Williams arpeggioed... to zero
below. You varied the tune. The Black Sea is cold.

3.12.22

194

All the world's a staging of *The Crossroad* : a play
– revenge melodrama, we should say – about greed
& envy & pride, mistaken identity. & we are mostly
merely witnesses. Like dreamers in a locked-door
mystery by Poe, whose feral beast in Paris is fusion
of enemy & alter-ego – so this nightmare screed
appears to offer no way out... no hope of dawn.
That raven, in his verdigris poplar, croaks *nevermore*.

So when I hear Prokofiev's tender, exalted aria
composed in Voronezh, I think of banished Mandelstam
just down the muddy road – hugged by Akhmatova,
his forlorn friend. One turns to idyll, one to epigram.

The violin vaults up vertically, orthogonal – on the octave
like a sing-song child, chanting : *Seek ye the Lord, & live.*

& how is it that Prokofiev, Akhmatova, & Stalin
all died on that same day, in early March? Tip
of a steel foil, blooded like these spring maple buds;
sweet coltish gait of Natasha Shtempel... *amen, amen.*

All the children sing in the youth choir, listen enrapt
to the tale of *Peter & the Wolf.* Each instrument
speaks for a character – Grandpa's bassoon,
soft fluttery Bird's flute, unlucky Duck's oboe, sly
Pussy's clarinet, brave Peter's string quartet... soon
Wolf's fearsome horns. Children, at the zoo, ask why
only Duck, in Wolf's belly, still warbles? Is still trapped?
Prokofiev wonders, too. Lips whistle from clay firmament.

3.14.22

195

On the cusp of March, we taste the season's seeming
        endlessness
here in Siberian, microcosmic Minneapolis.
Ice breaks. The rivers flow in four directions
toward the sea. George Berkeley, whom the Empire shuns
waits, waits, in Paradise... looks out toward wide oceans
of infinity. Each wave flashes a single flicker-syllable,
merged with the omega of its one vast azure unison
at the horizon (solid gyroscope-angle, masting galactic
        babble).

The indivisible unity of human happiness – a mystery
toward which Odysseus departs (O hankering Homer).
Nostalgia of Du Bellay; his fields, inexpressibly far away
from Rome. *Bella, horrida bella...* (each political
        misnomer).

There is no *Z* in Zeno, ominously. & the four *Y*'s
in Volodymyr Zelenskyy crypt a grail-King in disguise.

Beware the Ides of March. The density parameter
of universal mass is hidden in that box of keys
buried in Brazil jungle beehive – that breeze
in the key of *C* transmutes into a horseshoe's pair

of broken lips – crumpled Open City of an after-siege.
The graffito'd *Z* of Caesar's saboteurs & underlings
is backward obeisance to the Last Judgement
of men, of all their hollow, corrosive, iron things;
of all the thespian savagery of their weakling's rage,
of all bowing & scraping before his Imperial Dement.
Berkeley, in Paradise, waits at the center of the Rose;

where humans rise toward joy, there the *Son of Man* goes.

3.15.22

196

The ghost of Shakespeare was calling to me –
an old mole in the clay, on St. Patrick's Day.
Swear, by my word! *The steel scraped tinnily*
when I yanked it free, said the blithe King of May.

Some discord mars the key of Rus, mourned good Prince
        V.

I've just begun to fight, cried John Paul Jonah – *hip*
        hooray!
Like matryoshka dolls. A play within a play, a ghost
within a ghost. *The sea encircles Ireland*, my host
averred; *the Queen rides on her shell, to Restoration Day*.

                                    3.17.22

197

Great was the year & terrible the Year of our Lord *2022*
when, like a demon out of *Master & Margarita*
the Master from Muscovy pronounced his fetid word
& the horrific noise of fraudulence, with a *rata-ta-ta*
began to rain down on Ukraine – against the grain
of human heart, & brain, & hands, & feet – those smiling,
multifarious, weathered, dignified faces of tender pain...
– little demon, little obstacle to heaven, I'm talking to you!

Bulgakov, in *The White Guard*, like a hideous mirror
limned the siege of Kyiv, as in a painting by Holbein –
an immense, shifty skull at the foot of each ambassador
marking the limit of *raison d'état. Magnifique, nein?*

& Volodymyr, his brief entrance... (rhymes with
            redeemer).
So Hal tried on his crown, outside Jerusalem Chamber.

Everything is changed, everything transmuted
in those late pastoral romances of Shakespeare.
Accents of farewell. A simple wave of departure
(*goodby, goodby*). Ariadne, Ariel... wingèd, fluted.

Here, amid calm sleepy grain fields of Minnesota
the border of the sea calls me. A blue-black surge
(wave after wave) more calm, more relentless now
than Time itself – a *Judgement Day*, coming to purge
distracted representations, our politic know-how
into the spinal whorl of a planetary Ark (*amen, selah*).
Shape of your own soul, O infant Prince, O *Faerie Queen* –
Love's graceful realm... gentle, serene (maybe Galilean).

198

Spring inches slowly into Siberian Minnesota.
Yet today is mild. The pips of tiny infantile finches
or sparrows squeak, off-stage, through cedar slats
of my esteemed, Pushkinian (Oblomovian) gazebo;
the madness of the Czar grinds slowly, wrenches
innocent minds & hearts with familiar woe...
ancient, echoing, extravagant malice. Bad hats
scurry to Shakespearean ratholes. *O lacrimae*!

Your Byzantium, O Czar, is built upon a primal theft
bright Roger Williams skried, quite long ago.
Proposed his own high Providence, warped on a weft
of Chaadev's *moral freedom* – Cusa's learnèd *I-don't
            know*.

*It was not price nor money could have purchased Rhode
            Island;*
only *all-human companionship* (cosmopolitan,
            understand).

& you do not see as Roger does, O Czar.
Mankind is *Imago*, indeed – a wayward one;
YHWH-design's inscrutable. Not *Rus* empire,
nor *U.S.A.,* officiate for his belovèd son.

I remember the young forsythia's light sun-canoes
emerging, tentative & frail, in Providence
this time of year. & your flashing deep gaze,
your leafy wings, goldfinch; your mother's grave
at Swan Point (my father's birthday). Beethoven's
tremendous theme, hovering behind Osip's surmise
in Voronezh...*flowers are eternal.* Heaven is brave,

my child, my limping one – up there beyond these blues.

3.19–3.21.22

199

The people you meet in dreams make amends
for your mistakes, Henry. They love you
like the *purr-purra* of a woolen cat loves Sophie
when she's falling asleep, in an empty bed
on Sycamore St. (in Providence). *O the strong sea...*
so *Violet*, the State Flower, departs from red & blue.

Hold a wild pea against a sea-rose, Beauty –
we'll be leaving soon. All set. That droning overhead
is yon thrum of marching feet, marching to see
what the motors will decide. *Phoenix is dead*,
somebody said (all a-twitter) – *along with a turtle*,
those blue lenses are pure peacock (rustling myrtle).

I'm thinking of that man atop a bridge, on Washington
before winter ends, & I fall asleep too. He's thinking
of some Irish ghost among the shrouds – Melville, Poe?
Hobbling down Benefit, brooding on his girl, Whitman –
hops across Hope? *Enough, you blinking, drinking*
men! She hovers, elfin, over the clay... *shalom, shiloh.*

3.28.22

200

Jonah lay hunched in fetid, wheezy lightlessness.
Felt himself churned inside out, in his sailor's hat –
swallowed by his own hollow belly. Forest voices
ruffled, lisping, from some hoedown beyond whale fat.

What dream was this? Exchanged his navvy's togs
for a merman's diver-suit? They didn't want him
on board ship – a tongue-tied fling rimmed with bags
of ritual blubber, no doubt (by godly Ensign Grim).

He thought of distanced & evil Nineveh, now
with a curious yearning – her providential avenues;
tripping over his own callouses (& how!)
until, at last, a kind of limpid honey-dusk would ooze

from above – a silence of cornets. Like a dripping gum
from some immense, constellated live-oak candelabra
(sphered like curving smile in ocean mirror). Hum
to Galahad, vague, lambent whale... cloudy *Hagia Sophia*.

3.29.22

201

I paints my pictures to escape from abstraction, Hank
spake il maestro di color. *Blue ain't blank;*
blues a feeling. Was a fortunate shade in every photo
of the photographer (in Firenze, once); gravitational
lenses around lumpy galaxies allowed Earendel
to appear just above RI (by nearly a coupla billion
light-years, I guess). Matter of mirrors, O puny Human.

These color revolutions pose a problem for stormclouds
glooming around eastern sunrise, this time of year.
Red vs. blue, mauve against maroon... sunny yellow,
Syrian. A crimson tank trundles by (spring-loaded smear).

Our universal da Vinci capability is very positive
in a negative sense. *Thought of* Ground Zero?
– Keeps me humble, dude. Stuck there in costive
Genoa, Eugene pined for nut-brown Irma, like Hero
for her meandering star. Odetta sang, *I love you so...*
Right love, offspring of gleeful kiddish yearning, is
intelligible, incandescent. Is transcendent, Ariel (always).

*

In my heart there is a Providence, like a bird's-eye,
or bee's-eye, or bull's-eye view. Surrounds
my fallings down, refusals, shuttered guile; a sky
limpid with vanish'd morning dew, & spring bird-sounds.

A penny for Penelope, who threads the actual yarn.

Hues mesh, pastels comport & fuse into the future.
& you appear there as a figure in a timescape.

A dream-continuum, you almost turned to manure –
become composted from a better angle, tender grape.

*

Toughness crow in different ways. Cauterized
Henry-heart, used to the blows, suits up,
shrivels sometimes – *O yes*, he sighs
for his heaving Kedron. These memories,
like evening's April sunlight, the rusty silver
of a quavering robin's accolade... are more than all
the language summer's parked philosophy can't spell.

& the old criminals, out of ice-cold colonels –
but he just my age, that one! – Joey's double agent.
Meanwhile, the apostolic purple in Kiev will knell
cicada-doom across young hills & crumbly soil... *Repent.*

These late romances of yon April bard
shed a moss-green luminescence. Special hope
for ancient sparrows – flitting vulnerable shadows.
Odysseus, odd Duke in the mirror, finds it hard
not to be himself, after a while. Milan? Nope.
Headin' back to Gals, in my acacia Cadillac. 'Member?
Violette, *fleurette africaine*. Beyond red, beyond blue.

4.3.22

202

A tendril threads these chords of mixed-up memory.
Verdigris, I want you, verdigris – a *matryoshka* ghost.
That lean & wispy poet, with Jeff's girlfriend's family –
gleeful, brimful, *encantada*! Weathered as Oaxaca host.

A ghost within a ghost – like Poe in poetry
(uncanny photo, Providence). Wells from the past,
his father's footsteps on the rotten boards... *O Henry*!
Tossed like Jonah from the ship – nailed to the mast!

Aeneas carrying his father... one blind one's dream...
inextricable crossroads tangle, down in Memphis.
Keatsian Icarus was a nightingale Oedipus – cream
of Milky Way, wafting his Abelard from Red Sea blues.

& though Mabel Cain may have mothered Hannibal
& fiery Dido may have died, in Virgil's vein
yet acorn Hero bends a *Royal Oak* across her Channel
& the light charter of Earendel, no tyrant can contain.

4.4.22

203

The sweet immaculate *Snow Queen* out of Moscow
became an improbable children's hit in Japan.
& ol' Hank Halwick remembers *The Suicide* tubas, too
– at Trinity, in Providence; also *Life is a Dream*, up
in Cambridge (*La Vida es Sueño*). Even Stalin was a fan.
Our motorized legions will eliminate all pothole schemes

& the so-called citizens who dig them. Henry don't,
oh no. *Volga-Volga*, all the way. When Paul Muni
didn't get to play *Shark Island*? Was no crime
(though many were prevented). Don't be, guy,
worked up about Shakespeare, okay? There's no time.
Word from Bulgakov is, *Kyiv*. (Christ, bears the brunt.)

Seems you've entered a convo that has already begun,
little Judas Priest. The rats are in the building,
everybody's left who's left. She's tearing to see her son –
the Mariupol Countess (from St. Paul); something
terrible is happened. Linchpins rasping for Dr. Mudd
found just a penny in the dirt, smudged with blood.

4.5.22

204

I don't blame them for what they done to me,
sorry drunk that I am, sorry.
You can't play *Everyman*, Henry, until
you adopt all your neighbors – carry their socks
to the curb, smell their sweat, their character quirks
& feed each whole fold of my flighty-burden flocks –
was how barracks was ward, & Wells got wells,

in the Civil War. Evil is an uncanny force
marked by inhumanity, like a mask
without a face; & hearts must rise to the task
of rowing brooks back to their common source.

King Charlie in the oak tree was a youngster once,
but now he's old, old, Henry... flourishing his linden
penscript to a vernal breeze from Narragansett Bay.
& while baby violets will sway in the hurricane
up from Montawk & beyond – yet no force can destroy
what circuits down from perfect vision, to announce
these galaxies, my little Jesse tree, are goodly works.

4.6.22

205

The immediate life-death struggle, the constant strain
to orient oneself (like Odysseus, or that skittish king
up on the parapet) to inexplicable contingencies. Man!
– you kind of dud Siberian bog art, with scorpion sting...

There's somebody standing right in front of you, yelling
Wake up! *Come down, come down from your cold gold*
sleep mountain of snow! Who takes all the spelled-out
laws into hell-brain, muscle... & transmutes them – bold

as love! Williams, plain as a penny from Providence,
rolls back his *Ocean State*, like a Noah's ark –
back to Cherokee-lean Abraham, whose dense
pine-spine lifts *Constitution* from Potomac muck.

& I fell into your fishnet threads, Ariadne-Penelope;
I broke them beneath my weight. O seamless life
of vanishing dewdrops! Still the children play
beneath your billowy shrouds, light sister-wife!

4.8.22

206

The light is not mine; I follow the light.
As when the sun, behind these mottled April clouds
prolongs its time on Earth, as if waiting for me.
And the season flowers, full of memory.
The life was good, though these low-brimmed crowds
stir strange gatherings (spoiled for a fight).
& he not even king – some chest-pinched rabbi

from hinterlands of Georgia. O gentle realm
of absolute poverty! Children dance in the dust
behind a sharecropper's flimsy barn. Take the helm,
heavenly justice! Your law – David's trusting crust!

Providence was my home, beside a seaweed shore.
All my inconclusive memories are there – your word
of purple sea-rose promise... unblemished future
not yet come. A little microcosmos, in RI –
a dream, that's all. After the brimstone guile is gone,
the exploitation of mankind by man at last abjured
for good. Rise kingdom rose, kind Rabbi-sun.

4.10.22

207

Springtime in Hopkins, in my mother's paintings
anchors my heart, like Andrée's tugged toward the Pole.
Their early splendor enfolds all these Rhode Island things
(by Maxwell Mays, or Maximus) in one round clay bowl.

This crypt of April is dangerous & holy; here's the key.

From Abraham to Martin King there is a Union thread
wound tight around the bone. Keeled sundial, tiller of
       JFK...
grail-box from Camelot, for the American dead.
Come back to life. A Whitsun valentine (at end of May).

4.11.22

208

We, the peoples – how we straggle, each our local dialect!
Of trouble. In the solidarity of the castle
th'encircled satyr (McBeast) abhors such hair-
pin curves of orbiting entailment (them who perfect
the hedgehog round his crown). There's the eye
of the Ogre now, with his *ack-ack* confederates – hustle
to their doom. True prayer... only heave-a-sigh. *O rookie
       air.*

Smiles. *I have no wrath.* Bright motes of infinitesimal
           points.
Stringy Thierry strings along, like Ariadne labyrinth
of some uncharted *Notre Dame*; imperturbable ebullience
marks Nick Cusanus with a kiss (myth's *Loch Ness* plinth).

They pummeled Boethius for his beehive – his witty nest.
For the triangle of his quadrivium (*Union, Equality,
Connection*). It was a way of weaving song-reality
into new song; it was a yellow-black goldfinch (blest
nonsense, piped into a children's book). Poe... *try.*
The night runs toward the day, the sunrise – watch!
Your fathomless Scotch father's here (*tes yeux Byzances*).

4.12.22

209

A score from Samuel Barber, *Sure As the Night Shines*.
Slow octaves on James Agee, back to Crane (*Permit Me
Voyage*). Heart swims on saffron sky, over these pines'
sapphire, dark green... that yellow rose is *Charity*,
Henry. & the chair waits for Elijah, not for you
(*human American man*). Over swamps of Ravenna
the stars are still the same, your fortitude remains
– & she brakes by the bridge, dark-eyed sunflower (*Soo

Line*). Sophie might sing it one day (for piano, violin).
That melodious child-eye follows you everywhere, Cusa –
beside your *redemption that has already happened* (in
the key of *M*). Moving toward the octave (Mira, Natasha);
everything spherical moving through the clay, the rain.
Perfection of the common good is oneness, Boethius.
We know it as we sense thy equal tone (whole happy
heart). *It is finished,* Lincoln, Martin... Rose Lighthouse.

4.13.22

210

We started out compromised, Henry, anyway;
in the Florida clay, on the shady sand – no
Mayflower coast guard vessel standing by.
Feeding sharks kept us compact & expanding,
O Peto! (*Reminiscences of 1865*). A midget copper
Indianhead, Penny – for all this graven cedar door
can hold. A cypress grail (to wash your feet, Penelo).

In the mandorla... a wizened, rail-split Icarus, mayhap.
Amen, Abe. *Agape*. The clay releases these
many homegrown, useful Ulysses – *jolly good, old chap*!
Peto's civil boredom? Is perennial (*fado*, Brown
          Decades).

Yet somehow your slow, yearning Samuel Barber chords
maintain (from *A* to *G*) its octave for a reconciliation.
Old Masters go blind on the way home – but their words
were never utterly off. They came from the unknown
wilderness of heart's loafing – its maundy understanding.
With *malice toward none...* &... *of the people, by the
          people...*
so keys blend, toward a milky reunion (pink palm steeple).

4.14.22

211

A yearning to depart rhymes with sad evening light;
like a phrase in Samuel Barber's *Nocturne*, or the waltz
played by Slenczynska (*Let's Sit It Out*). Such bright
triplets belie the melancholy of grainlands,
this time of year. *You can biff me, you can bash me,*
but you'll never get it. Ruth plunked a better bravery,
Henry – she not your foe; yours not her favorite hands.

Not a secession, only a departure. Promise to return.
You'll need all 50 states for Jubilee – even the tiniest;
just so Jonah ran off, came back to Nineveh at last
after three nights. One hides in the land (in an urn).

Piero painted his *Madonna del Parto* on a flaking wall.
Nicholas invented a wobbly ball game round her womb.
These tears are the aftermath of each blind missile
strike – the desolation of these women at the tomb
your own, Natasha. & yet if Nicholas perfects
his toss... we'll find our own immaculate communion.
Our undying life – rose-fingered islet of reborn creation.

4.15.22

212

A giant comet, the size of Rhode Island, will hurtle by
in close proximity to Saturn's rings, & vanish
into nocturnal *Okean* (phosphor stream of space
& time) – signaling a new age for the human race.
Its enormous, silky, sable-golden tail will burnish
every planetarium, like Jonah pelted from the sky.

In ice-cold depths, the barracuda communes hum.
We must play fair – simple, all-human, planetary.
One law rules Saturn's rings & Hades' Styx. *Come
help me harrow Hell*, the tall Ghost calls – *for Jubilee*.

Your tiny *Ocean State* will not secede, but suffer
a sea-change (*full fathom five*). & we will not depart
but recommence, carrying the candle of the lowly king
of Providence – his ruddy-gold lighthouse of everything.
Just when the curtain falls, & Prospero abjures his art;
when sunset threads of Penelope stretch true, knot sure.

4.16.22

213

Sleet. When cold rain, warm slush turn lightweight
salt. Drifts across your April avenues, gray
Minneapolis. Bored with the horror of himself, *hey
ey yo...* turns to the Baal Shem Tov, in far Ukraine –
*seek the voice of the divine foreverness, my love. So near,
        so great.*
Only that Milanese romance... Eugenio, Irma (checkmate).
Oneness you know beyond Union, Lincoln. Man's salty
        fate.

Like the faded valentine that folds Oblomov's adoration;
a flimsy paper origami boat... his *Pallada*... his *Argo*.
Or like the set theory of Nicholas Cusanus : *so
to a crystalline circumference your circle tends, my son.*

So you behold young jolly Roger, of Rogue's Island –
all his piratical & pure good will, but a sailor's tattoo
of simple steadfast heart (rude beating rooster-clock
of Henry House). You are that cube of salt, that grain
of wheat, scattered over the rolling sea... so black,
so deep. You are that humblest coin, one rusty clue –
spring nimbus, hid in the ground; lost pearl in the sand.

4.18.22

214

Blackstone's oak, in Cumblerland, was in his mind's RI
the way Berkeley's bark anchored in Paradise (Newport).
Riding westward, on woodwinds… low scales & high –
thundering sky, & friendlier ground, & blue sea-bells.

One acorn leavens each loafer, light in her oaken arms.

So honor & affection draw thee near, my Everychild.
That hobgoblin Leviathan shall fade with day.
A deeper communion brims all-human glee; wild
Whitsuntide suffuses Birtwhistle – one shrill bluejay.

4.19.22

215

Pained aggravations of drag-yoke, doom-laden April
cloud heavy Henry (silky RI jerk) on thy gravy doings.
Plinks aslant him, Arthurian avenues – below that real
ol' Witch's Hat, his mother Mary's elementary makings
(Ukrainian *pysanky*, once... with gentle bunny-chicks
at Sydney Pratt). Put all your eggs in one Stillwater
mirror, Hen. Mariupol may rise. Translate (*traslunar*).

Your friendly ghost be more than a *Shmoo*-in, kid.
May be *Argo*-eyed, altogether. May be the singing
Black Sea keel herself (authentic Hagia Sophia bling).
More things, Horatio... Swan's eyes? Knot you too, kid.

Departs haunted, staged, right... May happy returns!
Posthumous, from the humus first (humorous!).
After that lastful measuring cup, & quaffed with mead
this high – from a goldfinch yolk, from a promise
rose a Newport berth (for *Freedom*). It was a vernal
prelude... it was a green bounce off that whole, deluded
Globi-orb... it was a little skippy skiff (John F's *Tock*
            Ticks).

                                            4.20.22

216

The Ukrainian kid in the tank turret
has taped up a photo of the *Hodegetria*
icon. *Virgin of Kyiv*. The secret
of the wisdom, that she points toward? *Hagia
Sophia*, wobbly vessel of her womb – an almond
bitter as the winter clay (elliptic *Table Ronde*).

We are shipping heavy weaponry as fast as we can
to this gravity vortex of nothingness. Only a whiff
of sulfur, vanity... envious theft of life
by Hell itself. Understand – *last full measure*, American.

A grain of salt in the soul purifies through suffering,
Henry. Hurl, God, your judgement against our keel
until each teardrop from her eyelash – each finger-
point aslant his hovering palm – is royal seal.
So the angel's flame scorches our bartered lips.
A woman at the gates waits for her son. *Neva*, the ships.

4.22.22

217

This little agate, found buried in the dirt –
a miniature mountain, with summit of quartz
& narrow rings of bronze – as on a whirling skirt
from Ilium, or Ithaka – is sealed by twin circlets
resembling a horsehair wedding band, or figure *8*
sketched by some calligraphic art; also a *Great
Red Spot*, Henry (reminder of unfinished business).

Imagine all the pebbles on the shore of every sea
whorled, somehow, within this weathered labyrinth.
Until its secret gate opens... & there you see
the finished *Sampo*, for example (launched May 29th).

On the Day of Restoration, so, *we shall not all sleep
but we shall all be changed.* In the twinkling
of a Rose Island Light (as in this remnant
from the deep). To climb like stones, awakening
from earth, & sea... like stars, no longer somnolent;
like ocean salts, becalmed within this Paradise we keep –
a sheepfold of equality (your *agape*, your *Shekinah*
        presence).

4.26.22

218

It was the 4th of July. It was a special Jubilee
for Tom & Jeff, chasing each other around the table
(blue-whisker'd cat, puffy red-check'd mouse). *We
have to get past this partisan cane-swinging, Abel –
hey?* The sketch is always a natural travesty
of better angels, Abe. Let's find our blind & blackt-
out way – back to the topspin of the topsail, Jack.

Counter-clockwise wheels the green clover
through the veil of Adam's grief;
her gyroscope, atop the sky, nods over-
head... (acorn amid the massed oak-leaf).

I have desolated my own kingdom out of lack-love,
howls the shocked Lear, that grand old fool;
out of petty spite, out of blind pride. Cordelia
forgives; forgive. Thus waves of the human ocean roll
through each shattered arctic heart. *We are* Sophia
with a million eyes, chants the caged nightingale;
only rise on these glazed wings, bewildered majesty.

4.29.22

219

That rose-breasted grosbeak, cut-throat bird
circles the feeder at sunset – shooing off
frisky chickadees, a keyed-up finch. *Poof,*
my gold *frère… adieu, mon coulombard.*

Still, your forsythia tosses her sulfur coins
over the gray rubble of a rustlers' graveyard.
Slobbovian cartoons grow brittle… awkward
icons, Henry, jerry-rigged. Try spare silence

for a change. You have to lose yourself
in pure devotion to the Providence you trust
to free yourself. *I have no guile*, chanted the mast
in the sea-wind – shedding fool's gold (nailed pelf).

Your Patina is calling you, O coppery king. Her face
is like her mother's, green man, Jack o' the green;
tears course the arc of her cheeks; she has been
through the wars. Your Word is but Cordelia's embrace.

5.1.22

220

There is always a backstory, Henry, barely flickering
in the abysmal backyard of your mind. That steep,
zigzag & faery *ghat*, down to Big Muddy (*deep
& strong*) where, sad, you descry your Maker, making;

& you recall your father, John, benevolent *apostle
of intellectual property to the Indians* (saving
rice grains from the corporate brand). Keeping
his icon, swaying, hot, happy & tired, by Taj Mahal;

remembering that other touched vociferous gospel singer
con geat & harp, who led you down his dusty path
of blues & rhyme. Love is the cure of wrath
& the healer's key – the grain, the turmeric, the zinger;

Love is the source of that great River, *Okean*
where Blackstone launched his coracle at Cumberland
by his *Catholic Oak*, & Roger found Canonicus his friend
& wove the pattern of an ancient amity, all-human;

& hidden in that trellis-work of leafy greenery
a faint, translucent circle – like a *mahamudra* (or
the phantom of some *Acorn Seal*) will shimmer there
for you, Henry... Penelope, unflagging still (still revery).

*

& like the roar of many chorusing waters
or a *Thunderbird* starting up from a massive tree

the glossolalia of a global euphoria begins to hum

as the lyre of Roger's islet strings together, catenary
& a child steps from the well of sons & daughters

*

His apologetics were, in truth, often apologetic,
the confessions of his confession; but Lil' Rhody
was set up by Roger to be a refuge for such as he –
waywards in exile, troubled by conscience... sick,

in other words. An Everyworm. & that enthusiastic
legal eagle feathered his rock-salty nest with a spirit
ecumenical, economical. The *law of life*, from the start
was for all, is for all, for one & all – vast, oceanic.

So the minimum state contains the maximum sea,
the middle *C*, the whole streaming galaxy – just as
Nicholas Cusanus, with his inventive helium gas,
patented the finding of the seekers... inwardly.

Just so your soul bobbled beneath the North Star,
Henry. Just so your nation veered from its path
of humane liberty, natural right. So heed the math
of your figural father... turn again to love's *Paramour*.

The invisible queen, the Jack o' the green, the ghost
in the human dome, with a million eyes... the eagle
of *Jehanne Mandorla*, hovering aloft each rose ingle...
these filigree a May King restoration (coast to coast).

5.2.22

221

That green man, with his old face, emerging
from the stone – with his contrite heart,
with his hopeful sigh, with his despair (for Spring,
for all them Delta things)... Now, Ariel; do your part.

In the kindly, forgiving, *Dells* part o' the wood
e'en Sycorax might come to Miranda. What says
that fool, Sir Henry? He notta been so good.
The isle's a-brim, *ma chère*, with violets – primrose.

I spied Caliban, in the shape of a Minotaur
spoiling the chess game of chaste Prospero;
he waved his wand, made his foe disappear...
Nothing, my dear. Brief sadness; dream-woe.

Was all done long ago. Nothing remains now
my child, can harm thee – the world's asleep
in Prospero's dream. Your green will only grow,
seedling. Full fathom five... deep speaks to deep.

5.2.22

222

Primavera so late returning... the snow line
barely melted into May. So, on the north side
of the Witch's Hat, Osiris prods his raggèd barque
as was his wont, of a winter day (Twin Citian)
& rackety Henry's home at last – where he used to hide
his infant head (in Minneapolis). Trusty *Argos*, ark
of faithfulness, wags one last tale... (unusually tired).

Sweet unity of doggèd vision, Berkeley knew.
Nothing remains untouched by your faery realm
O *Holy Fire*, O *Goodly Fere* – so take the human helm;
let your odd 3-legged Jack sing out... hail *all things new*.

Green island... sorrowing, revolving clover...
Everything returns unto the oaken scaffold of your
loom, Ariel, Ariadne. Into the vortex of your coracle,
Penelope. Light changes on the sea, at dawn –
a bloodrose flickers on the moist horizon
as swift dancers on the sand retrace its oracle
in snowy foam : a *horseshoe* (wrested from receding tide).

5.3.22

223

In all them weeks of his 3 score years & 10
since baby Hen disembarked his *Mayflower*, began
to reckon up his *Mahamuddy Big Agate* collection,
he has never made himself a Testament (*ni Grand,
ni P'tit*) – though he *will*, someday. As with all charters
& summons-up of the *booty politique...* one is, &
one will be. & as all 50 states are equal (2 *senex*
each), even RI has her sparrow Providence – her *Lex,*

et son Esprit. It was *refuge for troubled conscience*
for a fool flung from London, Boston... onto wintry
strand, alone; for a Renaissance guy (tho' perhaps pre-
or -posterous) who paid back such Narragansett tolerance

(canonical, from the beginning) to that *last full measure* –
one *Rose Island Light*, of lovingkindness (steadfast, sure).

Stock locks, barrels... *shall all be changed*, muttered
her one ripe remnant (Prospero). Oar thy wings
to the isle now, Ariel. *We are translated unto things
not found in my philosophy*, brit Berkeley stuttered.

Poetry, sweet limpid wingèd sprite, transmutes
the heavy dross of US. Back to its springing source
in, in... (in a sense). Goodness. With sound of flutes,
defeats the constructs of our evil days (*remorse,
remorse*) – plays out the late romance of your *aubade*,
old, bad Oblomov. Your valentines for Olga, Irma.
For Penelope, strung to her spinning Jenny (sad,
courageous). Grave, Sienese... (braids, heart). *Selah.*
                                        5.5.22

224

There floats, suspended, at the center of the universe,
a Someone, like that eagle, drifting swift & serene
across the Mississippi. For all that is in motion, everyone,
Hesheshkedee remains the fulcrum of all cantilevers
(Henry's mystery name for what cannot be named);
& the substance of this One is love, *agape*, *caritas* –
what firmly binds mothers to fathers, sons, daughters...
(as *Phoebe* is epitome of Moon's pale nimbus, framed).

& all the very difficult, cold, emotionless men,
all busted marble mock-ups, with all their satellites
in Goodwill, Texas & elsewhere, are but frostbites
o'er *Mindel-Würm...* cast-offs from your world-kitchen

that persists with its own hilarious radiance, belovèd –
May rays through blue-bells, violets, my *Shekinah, shaked.*

& Henry Hankovitch was such a one, O yes –
his Florentine firecracker duds, his Reb full-dress.
& yet your grace, your moonlit gravity (confess!)
repairs him to that galactic Galilee... *J*-spiral's bliss.

Hagia Sophia collapsed yesterday, but our Justinian
will put it all back. He too is but a brave simulacrum
of that scintillating guest, who promised to return –
who sums us up, whose *I-Am* is US, somehow... hm?
Closer to closure than you think, Hank-o, mayhap.
Thy Gravesend Sienese glance, Rebecc, undoes at last
all cockroach mustaches, their barbarous bombast.
Rose granite Narragansett lamps alight your victory lap.

5.8.22

225

Strange weather; the planet is troubled.
The wind is up. The sky broods,
thundering. Yuki's cat-wise – reads
the codes; his Witch's Hat simmers (bubbled).

To be home... sweet milk. An acorn, nestled in its oak.

No one knows just how the Earth is balanced
on its great see-saw with a small sea-rose.
Yet Roger recalled Coke's everlasting laws. One
Magna Carta curled up in all hearts; Cusanus danced.

5.9.22

226

In the confusion of the scrum, sister – the slugfest,
more or less two sides of a coin, love & wrath,
easily switchbacked, fork lightning. & Cassius Clay
changed his name to Ali, in the name of dignity
– *bam*, *bam* – you can't beat me no more, honky.
& if you discern cloudy *Jonah* there, in her nest
of eye-light... boy-god, this treason along our path
might fade. Toss apples, Atlanta cherry milk, Hen-ray.

In the cab they bonded. They had a mutual fever
of shotgun verbs, family shock, unmendable;
their woo carved in clay cuneiform, forever –
so that buried, yet they rise (from rustblade rubble).

You will heed the will of the great I AM, *America
when your lions lie down with the Lamb*, spake MLK.

Each sabbath is a remnant of that Jubilee.
My *Day of Rest* oration is a promissory note –
shreds of a token of a time to come, O Maggie
M; in my *Ocean State* each person has an equal vote.

You were our *Mayflower*, little Phoebe – & still are;
the moon, that hovers over Narragansett Bay
of an August evening, lingers in my memory
like the founding of Byzantium, on your birthday.
Its fall, on mine, only the flip side of that copper star
pulsing... *with malice toward none*. Motherly,
Venusian. In the harbor, there. Where the high fleet –
Ark, *Argo*, *Constitution*... cedar coracle... amass,
        complete.

5.10.22

227

Thunderstorm came through last night, might be back
tonight. Even out here in the Dullsville flatlands
we bide thy tornado, Lord – swings for grandstands
like lightning in Hopkins, sometime. Here at his shack
of eightfold Oblomovian origami, ol' Hen thinks on,
& on... recalling that lesson of little J. Rhodian
Less-&-Lesselbaum, on the wee *mandorla* of Piero
della Francesca... swelled canvas of *Madonna del Parto*...

Dance around Mary, 'portunes that faery old gent –
dance around Mary. Love's topspin tops thy pin-
oak with pine, & such a hurry can speed to a thin
mantle of *motionrest*, murmured Iosif of Ghent
(otherway known as Nikki of Clues). *Her secret, ye
cheermen, sits on the bridge of* Nobody's Nose, *e'en yet*.

Look up to my old gal Olga, now – straight through
the matrix of this wheezy gazebo, muttered Rusty
Pete (high noon o'him *Day-Rest* motel duration); blue
as those eyes full of light, rimming *Hagia Sophia*... see?
The riddle's in plain sight. Just knows, for miles. &
so her ineffable *Mona Lisa* viability shimmers with smiles

& what was a *Game of Spheres* for Nicholas entails
a globeful of human joy (after all them lightning hails).
We will recognize the humility of the gray seashell
& the meekness of the unaccountable pebble,
whose interior yawns with a terrifying spiral, now –
a fiery windwhorl, like a gol-dang *Paraclete* meadow
hoisting us to the rose core of a coracle oracle
(in an excess of gleeful ecstasy). Lil' acorn miracle!

228

to C.G.H.

The moon turned pale russet, just a few nights ago.
In the shadow of the Earth, a lone pebble.
A bloodrose, sailing through silence (high, far).
Kuusisto performed *The Lark Ascending,* at SPCO –
one songbird's tender, ethereal sky-treble,
soft as human violin can be. You gave us both your
tickets, Cara (after plummeting scales, shattering knee).

Pekka follows that yearning skylark, higher & higher,
over serene may-flowers, poppies. Our circling calls,
our cardinal mimicry... powerful 8th-notes, in a choir
of extra-perceptive sympathy (passes through walls).

Henry's earth-bound, compromised clay versifying
ineffectually crumbles on, along. The hard men
do their cold things to the commonweal (the bought-
&-sold). You were born dark & comely, *sister-dove* –
on Constitution Day. & I built my own glue-drying
replica, my bird's-eye view of Maxwell Mays' domain.
Groin-wound; penny-burial. *We all shall rise & float in
        love.*

5.23.22

229

The sea writes her lines, & then erases them.
In the beginning was the wave (*I am, I am*).
Penelope (Ithaka, Providence) repairs her hem.
He wonders back to her, odd Hen (*vox clam*).

The sky is falling. Earth is rolled up like a scroll.
George Berkeley larks in Newport puddingstone.
It doesn't matter. Everywho *contains the whole*
(who's everyone). *Vida es sueño*, to the bone.

Earth awaits the intelligible glossolalia
of your audacious incorruptible child, Marie;
the one who sums up all the facets of *realia* –
qui chante the One beyond the one (*mais oui*).

Off stage with all but kindness, now.
Blue slanders… courteous in private, though.
Henry keeps yearning for the perfect show.
Not Yeats, not Keats? It's Prospero, somehow.

5.24.22

230

My special Providence, my special Rhode Island.
With your Rose Island Light, with your sea-washed air.
In the fall, small leaves from the great gray beech
are gold. In spring, pink, showy apple-petals scatter
like downy snow aslant the universe. & *One* will stand
under your understanding, always. Always within reach.
Agape, deeper than wisdom – humility's clairvoyance.

This wants thought (while the groin bellows, the belly
groans). It may come; & I won't make it out.
Ripeness is all, Horatio. Our Williams penny,
our Lincoln gift... kind *MLK*, that comes out right.

A pint-sized carrack bobbed toward the London stage;
its cargo a prince of the blood, marked for the gallows.
Yet the command, scrawled on his heart's page –
manumission, by the wax-red seal of that sparrow's
phantom father – translated metamorphosis of State.
Just so meek Roger's chart of CARITAS, compassionate,
became *C*-chords of Ocean-harmony (bright prescience).

5.25.22

231

Have you solved the riddle of the Messianic secret?
Have you opened the doors of the sea?
How many gold fish will Yule find in her net
when he teleports back to Penelope?

In vacant centers of a diamond mandorla, a rose has
        bloomed.

My weaverbird, the Lady Berkeley of my nest,
your dream was knotted with a special quiddity.
Its thread is rest... its rightful *akme* is all rest.
& mercy is just this (soft-curling shells' equality).

5.26.22

232

You won't get many halcyon days like this
in a Minnesota May; maybe threescore & ten
in a lifetime. Old Hen, with the bloom off
in his whack-rickety gazebo, recollects the bliss
among exotic trees of Providence. The rough
magnolia limbs, exuding their voluptuous flesh-tone
flora; the imperturbable elephant-trunks of beech
shading their circle of earth below, with majestic
wavering, Pharaonic fronds of floating green...
the nearest thing to Paradise he's ever seen.
& he recalls those Tibetan monks, with plastic
cups, pouring their transient mandala. A beach

of sand come to its intricate, serene apotheosis –
on vacant concrete, beside the Woonasquatucket,
crafting a supernatural seal of infinite spacetime
(in the mode of humility, in the key of beseeching).
Compassion is the skeleton key, *my rude Henry*
(wheezed his pal Johnnie B) *to the Shield of Achilles*
(heal), *to the Twelve Tables of this Roman racket –*
your own life, *my son*, *my son*. To cry oursel's awake
while we sing in this wood full of snow, lead, crime.
Reach a hand into the wound like flint (streaming
bullets, blood). What kind of demented school are we,
USA? Blind blasted boast, are we? & this... their wake?

It was mercy, & remercy (seeker, journeyer).
It was *malice toward none*, it was the end of wrath
rhyming with death – which, dyed in Ariadne's wonder,
is no more. Plunge into plangent combers of her bath.

So. The Twelve Tables. Of a 13th State.

Lucky (*free*, *Black*, & *41*) – to miss a bullet
(*taking cover*). But you know, it's never over –
the *natural law* of the heart, that is. The human
fate. The foreigner, the other... she's your lover.
Why? Because your families oppose each other
in a lovers' quarrel. That's the world (deluded
globe). On the hilltops, claymores clash... men
rival with each other for the chivalry of rivalry,
O Hen. *How I would have gathered thee, Jerusalem*!
But you would not. Note how the fig tree is denuded.
Yet mini-states lead unto *Ocean*-mind (Ariel's hymn).

Ireland... Dean Berkeley, under his pilgrim exiled oak
in Paradise. On his puddingstone throne. He'd like
you to meet himself, in person (*for so lorn*). He says
there's a Person of all perceptions – hinge of the spoke
of *Hagia Sophia*, *with a million eyes*; she sits beside Lake
Placid, weaving a tapestry for unicorns (yourselves).
He understands (by clues of Kues) the *Goodwill Games*;
he plays ball – a ball of yarns. Yet there's a sound
penetrates through every wall... every mound
of clay. It is the murmur of a *Thunderbird*, beyond
all names. It is the sighing of the sea, its middle *C.*
It is the love you bear with me, *SK, Sophie, Alex, Phoebe...*

FT.

5.27.22

233

Hwæt just a minute! squawks Hen. Hear ye, all youse!
The May King, the *Man Who Did Not Deliver*, is
delivered is – delivering – her Child! & he is making
it (*his* way, with all the macaroni) toward his Throne!
I'll walk back to the sky, he sez, *through Hamlet's own
grave-groaning mill-race... unto Ophelia* (her happening).
Upon her lips, the graceful pathos of a children's song;
her memory's a general *Whitsuntide*, before too long.

It is this tragic wail from buried-mean Osiris
touches each feather on the scales. The lizard,
the judge, the cops, the banks – the law's delay (*oyez*)...
monstrous Oedipus is blinded. Life is hard

in Minneapolis. Washington St. shimmers over ice.
Old man, my son, my self... accept the King's advice.

She is lowly, Mary. Open as a child. He is in disguise.
Gnosis of *kenosis* guides her, to the downward slope;
*harlots & the tax collectors enter first, O Pharisee*s.
He's our embodied *Ima Go 'Thee* (hope, hope, hope,
          hope).

The green man of the oak was hidden in the leaves.
Like JFK, swaddled on his dealt-out deck (stiff
skiff, blithe skipper). Like Peter the Great (still
innocent, disguised) slipping round the docks at Delft.
& Dean Berkeley, & Bishop Nicholas of Kues... will
human intellect prevail (by way of inventive Kyiv)? – *'s
possible*. In the high room, in a circle of soft fire
the *whfft* of Ariel sang out... from unison to choir.

234

Henry, with his raspy prophetic yawp
over love & law, the funeral of tenderness –
studying (with fearful shakes) the Finnish rune
of his own ruin – Henry, wiresome irascible bored
Baudelaire, snarling at every shopkeepers' top
job (new reading glasses?) until he died – soon, soon.
Ah, him glum Minneapolis sadness, him trapped remorse!
Christ! cried a guy at the crossroad. *Motherlode...*

Ruby, my gnarled cedar neighbor from Montgomery,
was a child when MLK walked down the street. *Mind
your chores, children – help your Momma. See
you do all your homework, too.* Be not forever blind,

my heart. So Hen begotten up one day, posthumous puss,
& walked... & saw trees walking, too... walking for *US*.

What is MAN, *that Thou art mindful of him*? *Of her*?
That is the question for today, children. *'Tis not Rome,
the city, but Man's place in the universe.* You're home
                sure;
& that *Whitsun One* done come already, son. Come

again! So light played like a smile on the curving lips
of *Hagia Sophia*, bending down on brilliant wings –
filling your heart & every heart with a good ship's
worth of hopefulness, *coraggio*. Because the things
that are infinitely small (like my dream of *rd... rd...
rd'island*) contain the infinitely vast, the immeasurable
endlessness of shining stars... within your heart, noble-
humble sailor – *Jonah*-dove; wistful *coulombe*; sweet God.

235

Out of Egypt she came, sweet fool, her swift feet
drumming the sand with her desire. To the Tomb.

Our paltry words cannot master the immanent *Power*
(invisible, indivisible, ineffable, constant, serene...)
molding each living shape in that bright womb
of rosy fire – whose flame no icon can out-sheen.
& yet we find this spray of lilac in our cap (her flower).

Our *Royal Oak* is but a coracle. Thine infinite sea-comb
skims to the touchpiece of each soul (so quick... so fleet).

5.30.22

236

June. The air is sparkling clear & breezy as a mind
should be, not near so jejune as blind ol' Henry
Pussy-cat – squandering round, batting his giant
Braille of yarns to mangled spideywebs, dusty
as history. The word was *seek & ye shall find* –
because the omnicosmic *Yam-Power* within this tent
of blushing neighborhoods is indeed the May King's
Son of Woo-Man – yodeling Imogen of *Makes-Her*
             Things!

The heart knows, & the pure deed of selfless love
unfolds, out of remorse, like a rose-petalled parachute
lifting your whole being into its lofty, origami alcove –
finding clear encompassment (with mercy at its root).

One valentine rose, in its desert urn of far-off eras
sheds gold bee-pollen from a heart beyond the galaxies.

Uneasy murmurs – Scots, Aramaic, Japanese...
Henry's cat-talk, mewling at way-far train hoot
across high lonesome Appalachians... those *keys*
that open a box of keys (O happy-yappy shade-galoot).

& the shady tent was like an acute triangle
off a Federal mansion, flopped into an Ocean State;
from the belly of a mobile pyramid – that mummy
trove unearthed just yesterday, with a jingle-jangle
in the stone door hinge, the linty lintel of a potentate –
came the precipitate coherence of humus-entanglement;
in the ire-eye of a hurricane, in the game djinn-rummy
of behovely Roger's will – his Pen's *warp-keep-u*
             testament.   6.1.22

237

Motion of night air in Minnesota
sheared off the top half of an old bur oak
by Lake of the Isles – leaving a forlorn stump
(*Paul-Bunyanesqu*e?) teetering skyward. Just another
bump on a winter bridge. But with an "epistemic take
on humility", the artist reaches up, further...
as when that sparrow of Maxwell Mays will eye
all commingled emerald crowns in one *Cat Swamp*.

Most of my pencils are sharp, anyway. Those
roses of dawn, those evening pearls, are nothing
beside soft-waving ferns... these graceful palm-fans
of galactic phenomena. So *la mia cattedrale* takes wing.

Your firmament is beautiful, Agnes – simple as a walk
on salty sand. It is an Ocean State (beyond all talk).

So the *Word* that was wrapped around a shell
unfolds itself – unfurls its shell... the fern waves,
the wave fans. Life's restored again, lifted from hell.
Grace hover over thy canvas, *sea-folk* (dove-braves).

The stoicism of a solitary soul in search of dignity –
soul liberty (hers, his... theirs, ours) – is fused
within a photon-wave of commonweal, the simple good
we share – built upon a plain, incomprehensible triangle
(*Self-Other-Love*). Sweeter than honey-gold, brighter
than natural law... better than Sir Edward Coke, even.
I stretch this limb of a haunted pine toward your
palm, Penelope – heart's Providence (*kingdom of heaven*).

6.4.22

238

It was the harvest time, it was oak-apple time,
it was the end of the end of May in every galaxy;
in every hilltop hamlet, it was the Jubilee
for good Queen Liz; Charlie, & Mary too, was there
with the whole gang, upstairs, in Jerusalem. &
for old John, in Easter candleflame, tremble, my prayer.

It was the Feast of Weeks, all 52; my two-tone tulips
place *totafot* upon your brow, meek dream dreamer.
Your sons & your daughters shall prophesy
& even the crude rhymes of a roodster from RI
may (*re* Pentecost) repent – when He shalt float Her
one whole *Whitsun Ghost*, athwart a fleet of Noah-ships.

& you that battle with each other, endlessly
for the rough shadow-crowns of power an' glory –
know there is a Prince in this hamlet, bears *something
dangerous* for thee upon his heart. He is the king
you fear, the laird of poverty & righteousness;
your soul awaits his *Rose Street* ban, his Inverness.

6.5.22

239

Morning came, like my dear in the night breeze
out of a dream of headlamps in the grave.
Her face, while curtain shades convexed (concave)
gave forth a quietness, calm, Sienese.
Day's not-yet-gilded bilocations of catastrophe
floated... ineffable photon-quanta (lonesome, solitary).

Old man, have faith to lose yourself, again – *O
Hen Blueheart*! Toward vast, octahedral *Middle Sea*
of mingled lingos, outré caravels – Rhody,
Dhaka... your scrimping neighborhood, barbarian.

Whence cometh this light morning air, Cordelia?
Mine eyes are blind. I know it not. My kingdom's
captive as clay horsemen in a cave. *Accidia*,
confused dispute... these carve our grave. Kind Williams'
balanced on his Kedron prow, in Providence. Stiff ghost,
upright – hand still outstretched. LOVE is our host.

6.6.22

240

That high society, famous of newspapers & magazines
for which our painters & musicians ply their trade
shocks all provocables, adores a thing well made.
Cocteaus, Picassos & Stravinskys make the scenes.
Everyone cheers when tennis champs are on parade;
hinged marionettes obey the tick-tock's cruelty.
Political coyotes fidget for their prey.

Henry mulls over his foggy Isle of Mull,
waiting for silver needles through the oak.
A thread of lightning. Silky hair on Golgotha.
Flint tickles the iron rim of Earth's wheel-spoke.

The smile of Leonardo mimics that of Mona Lisa,
traces her sine-curve circling the limbs of Man.
My graphene graph is smaller that a grain of sand,
thinner that *matière Bretagne*, light as a sigh. Yet
Nicholas of Kues, Dean Berkeley, felt the Master's hand
in Ariel's rhodoran air, *purpurring* tenderly in Mind.
Their *Ocean State* is infant laughter; seek, you'll find.

6.7.22

241

You, under your blanket of hoarse prayers
think of first wife, son; silk-stringed affliction
of Issa; stoic Japan. Under a horde of woes,
who can mime that calm nitidity of *Son of Man*?

She is a rose on the flaking wall of Madonna del Parto.

My tongue's nonplussed by the oneness of your fold.
The shadowy arrows of simple good will. These
fern fans, curving over urn & sepulcher, hold
One who's with us; *is* us. Cradled, floating in the reeds.

6.9.22

242

In Paradise (now a bird sanctuary, near Newport)
a jagged cleft in the shoreline forms a puddingstone
ravine – a valley of dwarf oaks & rhododendron
with clifftop panorama of Atlantic sapphire (infinite).
Under a shady outcrop, Berkeley would meditate, &
wait for his Bermuda dream-trireme (that never came).
His Paradise was like a mellow replica of Peter's Gate.

Alaska sported an actual *Bridge to Nowhere*. Rhode Island
proffers, instead, a fictional *Bridge to Somewhere*. Like
Crane's hushed middle *C*, it holds.... floats American mind
beyond irascible self-betrayals, toward the blue lake

of sky. A summer goldfinch rested on the chicken wire.
Joseph, forsaken by his brothers, will still recall
her winged, sunlit arrow-flight... eliding lower, higher,
loopy with undulating *portamento*; her hypothetical
apotheosis (out of the rubble of tyrannical
desecration of Kyiv) – for the honor of your Name.
Equality-Union-Connection... Sophia's *eucharist* (for all).

6.11.22

243

Hen, there are more things, my rational whore,
than are found in thy sky-high-pitched philosophy
of blues. The red thread of Rahab's charity
led to her walls' tumble-down – & furthermore,
Jericho is, forsooth, a fishing port in lil' Rhody.
That island rose of your flighty prose is EROS, too,
my Deer – ha' dropt in the greensward just for you.

& thus my Origen is clipt, as he might as well be. We
all smolder for it (e'en Tex MacCullough, in his tree);
so you, magnanimous rulers of trim shacks, be free
wi' kindness & mercy – because the superflux is we.

& your Alexandrianism, Sir Henry, is just plush vanity
in the melancholy, Flemish, blue-eyed, flaxen-haired
despair of thy princely son. Charley-horse Charlie,
always waitin' in the wings of a lead-month Scorpion's
brittle cloud-struts. Those black moods you mothered
from his Ariadne... arachnid Penelope... Fate's wounds.
For this, O Henry Rose, you maze be electri-chaired.

6.12.22

244

No man's an island, spake the poet-priest, & yet
each one unites both path & flower – is, somehow,
a RHODE. Your *Restoration Day*, Henry, will start
within the shiftiness of your own heart. *Sweet*
lonely sycamore off Broadway, little tree of sorrow!
Blinded by dry lust, like an oak-gall hornet.

Across the globe, the slaves of death
tarnish the human *imago*, feeding their fear & pride.
Hang the scapegoat in a tree, surrounded by dogs
& guns. Slosh their bestial complacency with shrugs
for the limbless & the weak. Our world : don't hide.
Yet *thy ketch will sail*, declares the carpenter of Nazareth.

I still smell the salt in the humid air of Providence.
Her scent of seaweed shores. I see the grainy gray
downtown... I hear the knock of Penelope's shuttle
threading a soft sheep's rainbow (tender, subtle).
So Piero's *Madonna*, & my gyroscopic Penny, say
– *Ocean's* Golden Gate *is open* – *let* US *dance*.

6.13.22

245

We've passed mid-June, Henry. Flowery summer
& retrospect. A brave wind fleeces Oblomovian gazebo,
carries off his paper valentine, for Olga... all the way
to Pushkin's dacha. *That is poetry.* So light & airy,
making room for yesterday's tomorrows, high, low...
gone. Unless you too can build a monument, Sire!
Outlasting oligarchs, con-men, pretentious brass.
Something to put the arrogance of power in its place,
since every serf & slave is good as you. *All men are grass.*

Cornered, immured somewhere (southeast of Kremlin)
Alexei Navalny is only a mile from Avalon.
The grail floats, high as *Hagia Sophia with a million eyes,*
just overhead. *Your* sense of rightness *never dies*!
Osip & Jonah both cry out – like mighty iron bells in Kyiv.
The smelting of that massive *kolokol* (in *Andrei Rublev*)
is but a mini-icon for the *Restoration of the Earth* –
when the *One-who-comes* to lead the royal *eyre*
– the judge, *Everyone-Bloom* – berths back in Eire

& everywhere. The sea, *hoo-hoo*, sings along with the air;
Ocean rhymes with *galaxy*, whorls fleets of stars
(with topspin) into that implacable hum of darkness
shrouding our incandescent home. & we – who are
at ease in the *Promised Land*, trusting in Mammon
& hypocrisy – recall : our King was a lowly man.
Servant to janitors in Memphis. When he cried, *the Ark
of history is long, but it sails toward justice...* Henry's
     Penny Hope
was harbored there. Her *law of love.* So give it scope.
         6.16.22

246

Sophie & Phoebe are preparing for departure –
back to Rhode Island, where they both came from.
Back to Providence, where they were born.
Penelope, their mother & grandmother,
waits by her loom of joy & sadness – while her son
stays by another shore (where Golden Gate winds hum).

The human heart is prickled like a porcupine – pickles
in the brine of its drab deeds, dull thuds of its blind
self-interest. What we want, fickle boy, we shall have.
One is good, the Father only, spake the former slave.
O milky-black Rabbi… alway druv down by them unkind.
Tiny white rows, on baby green. Swords rust to sickles.

Sophie will hunt for seashells again, maybe a horseshoe
buried in undulating sands of Odesa-time. Lucky
to live in this resounding, hollow galaxy – this curve
like the breathing breast of a great basilica. Swerve,
marvel with me, Sophie : this *Ocean* is for both plucky
& shy. One *sea-continuum* nurses undying love for you.

What you hear's not me, but the ring of something
buried in the earth, & long-forgotten. Maybe
a copper coin, a Lincoln penny, turned impossibly
silver; maybe the thrum of some ineffable wing
still sparkling mirror-showers of rainbow dew
flashed by, like *Rose Island Light* (Narragansett view).

6.18.22

247

Today the day stretches its full length, & orioles
glitter in the leafy shade (like Chinese mandarins)
& the great sun burns at yon majestic height – only
to turn... downshift, toward day's diminishment.
So antique poets contemplate the processional display
of mortal things. Actors, in time's panorama – *fools-
for-a-day* in some rustic *Ancient & Horribles Parade*
(at Chepachet, RI, on the 4th of July). Skins,
sweating through their *Purgatory Chasm* (all homemade).

I remain *as per*, in my steaming gazebo-turned-sauna
like some withered, shrunken Minneapolis Pushkin
or better, orotund Oblomov, versifying letters. *Ah*,
& *oh*, & *ya vy lublyu*, Olga. Dream songs, grown thin.
JB wrote sometimes about little animals, in his tent
of sweat – baby rabbits, bats. Here, my catalpa grows
toward shade... gnawed at by trickster chipmunks
(snapping young shoots). At its crown, tendril-flowers
wave in heat-waves. Farewell, far-fabled mountain monks.

I have lived these rolling years, three score & ten.
& like that other Petersburg poet, whom I met once
in Providence (brought him a plastic winecup; he offered
to take some poems back to his hotel) I would have poured
forth continuous gratitude unto your OCEAN
          FUNDAMENT
O Lord... if my heart were right. But you can afford
my grave mistakes. *Only have mercy, according to your*
          WEIRD.
Henry just mimes your *Ocean State* – & Henry is a dunce
who knows your *Paradise* will bloom, in restoration.
          AGAIN.

248

*It is difficult, yet we want to believe in the victory
of civilization.* – Viacheslav Chernukho-Volich

An evening breeze carries off the suffocating heat
of midsummer's day. Air in the creaky cedar gazebo
grows temperate again. The Opera House in Odesa
is open once more – booming with *Tosca* & *Turandot*,
with solemn unison branching to contrapuntal arias,
many-streaming river-chords. & I remember delicate
seraphic Professor Alexander Weinstein – Odesa refugee
at age 15, in 1903 : who welcomed me to Cambridge
for Thanksgiving, 1970 – playing his violin, reciting
        poetry...

Hatred & war cling like a virus to our differences;
the infinitely multifarious variety of thriving life
stirs resentment within the prison-house of cold
lack-love – malign indifference, indifferent malignity.
Brutality & barbarism are there, just over the ridge;
yet the wave-curve of these architectural harmonics,
this lyric atmosphere, lifts minds toward humanity –
hearts toward a new mode of equality. Enter the fold,
then, child – such *union* is love's *unison*, beyond all strife.

Arch beyond arch, wave beyond wave. Once again
I see Nicolas von Kues, sailing from Constantinople
& suddenly I know – my own imaginary little Rhody
is no different from all our other humanized percepts.
It is the imagination which invents that azure pledge,
& reconciles – within its partialities, its mirror-reality –
the *infinite*, the *perfect*, & the *good*, for all people.
& we await thy enfolding grace, to fill these precepts
with your truth – O *Immanence* of our own restoration.

249

Another serene quiet superfine summer day here
in this world full of storms. Such weather's
conducive to awes & meditations. Like to be,
I would, in Como Japanese Garden again – where
my mother (ancient muddy maker) would volunteer,
whose moss-moist thumbs merged the clay so diligently
through grey granitic sand. & there were 5 worlds
JB considered long, over there in Karesensui. Whose
center is omnipresent? Whose circumference nowhere?

The Baptist, a kind of Dead Sea Roger Williams
ate locust beans, honey – wuz a voice far-hollering
across bewildered sandy hills. *Make straight the way...*
The change, the new life, must be a transposition – key
to key – from *all about bodily M*e, unto *Spirit of Thee*,
somehow. & the realm of heaven must be a showing-
forth, right along through the wrung-dry streets of gritty
Providence (the city). Sparkling metaphysical clues...
you might solve that playful riddle, when the *Perfect*
                    comes.

As Nicolas of Cusa scribbled, we inhabit a human cosmos
made out of our own cardboard conjectures. The mind
measures; the heart is deep as *Ocean River*. Mine
is but *Zhen Xian Bao*, a little paper box of yarns – rose-
red as summer evening clouds, high over Narragansett
                    Bay.
& the global game is just a ball of yarn, *De Ludo Globi* –
twirls through 9 rings of sand, like Beatrice's arctic blues.
Your girlish unicorn, at rest in that stairwell on Savoy.
Graceful yarn, unending life... when mourning turns to
        joy.   *6.22.22*

250

That cliff's-edge statue on the heights of Providence.
Hieratic '30s effigy of Williams. Arching back,
slightly... upright as Easter Island Narragansett chief.
Like a blind *Seeker* stepping from his prow, one palm
hovers – for blessing, divination, admonition (*thus
far, no further*). Balances reason, mercy, & belief.

My poem is the testament of one Rhode-Isle enthusiast.
Think Henry in Dublin (with a grail of whiskyfied honey)
reciting *sages in their holy fire*... full of Yeatsian hot air
& shriven scrivening. Yet Williams was, also, *Baconian*;
free inquiry of questing intellect was his sole Phoenix-gift
for fumbling, misapprehensive *us*. Wisdom comes last.

What sets his Providence apart, at last? One firm
line – between *Spirit* & *State*. Conviction
of conscience is sacred liberty of liberties : no force
of mob or dictator, no puffed-up pretence of authority,
no fetid chauvinism of entrenched majority, can hide
the rootless, brutal dullness of each fanatic yahoo.

My little birchbark poem seeks a wave-washed equilibrium.
Wide *Ocean State*. Williams' *two tables of the law*
stem from one loveworn, lively universal law (human,
divine). You hear it in your heart... because its hum
already harmonizes there. Like hymns from Memphis,
or Byzantium. Like M's *Redemption* (which has already
      come).

6.24.22

251

The arcs of this firm, glistening rondure
arrayed in elliptic parallels, are mother-of-pearl.
Smooth ivory. This carapace, borne to endure
is hollow now. No footbeats. Merely a shell.
Lifted to your ear, the captive sea's refrain
whispers to your heart, as from an infinite well.
She threads a figure of love's universal reign,
somehow... & now you never want to leave her.
So when butterflies take flight, their shells remain.

*

You saw the shape far off, at the line of the sea.
It shifted & banked, like a sea-bird trying to fly –
puffed & collapsed, as windward turned lee.
A sail... it was a lost sailor, come home to die;
perhaps Odysseus, or some other weathered salt.
Ashore, you watched its flickering semaphore reply.
I am your spouse, Penelope – patient to a fault.
With Ariadne's wool, I wove you back to me.
My rose on dark sea-bed shall be your vault.

*

Waves murmur in my sleep... Homer ruffles the sheets.
It is a deep-droning unison. It is a galactic sea-law
at the center of the keys; what it begins, it completes.
The marble domes arch overhead, with human awe;
the luminous incorruptible *Word* manifests its worth;
yet the surprise *Thou* hast in store, no one ever saw,
no one ever guessed. *It is the redemption of the Earth.*
No proud Machiavellian force can perform such feats.

The pilot *Love* floats everything – from woe to mirth.

6.25.22

252 : CODA

Dragonfly gon' fly. Robin she warble in a tree.
Or maybe oriole? May be. Oblomov moon to her...
come back to me. Surely, Olga, she murmur.
Sure. Time rides her summer carousel (reality) –
ol' guy remembering Irma, branded in Brindisi.
Christ stop in Eboli; Francesca too. Cats purr
in Napoli – deepdown pagan futility. Don' matter,
dragonfly. Gon' fly like fire, hon – you'll see.

A thin high-soprano squeaky cry, like scrape of piccolo
on steel. Step apart from the muttering flocks,
yabbering exponential multiplexity! Carouse rocks
tonight, this crowd. Chariots of Ezekiel, O –
them wheels a'glory, Irma, Irma. Passin' over you
from here to Ferrara, smokin', smokin'. Hallelu.
Yo – sit right down in that empty chair, Henro.
We got nowheres else to go, groovy plastic chauffeur.

A far flute insinuates among these yappety birds.
Some sweet kid's iron camouflage, like a *farfalla*
afloat over tigers. That Sam Barber fella...
curly-headed, yet. No close shave, no afterworse
for Ariosto (this time) – he just a sigh in otiose
RI, I guess. Sleepyhead, adrift. Hawkfeather
let fly, by wing – from *Mr. Alexander Pushkin Raptor*,
could be. Goldfinch, *nyet* gloom. Nightingale. Pathos.

Just a jay, with usual pines. Power & cruelty
mind own's mirage, surly unwisdom; goes away
with a father's kiss, only. Maybe another day,
Junior. Give a call from the Kremlin, K? – we'll see.
That lady with name like *dove* embodies poetry.

She stand outside the castle (weakened legs, firm
lips). It's everything that passes through – the storm,
wing-fans overhead. Huge hand reaching down (Mary

R. Good... pained, painting). I can show you this,
JB – from Minneapolis! See the grain elevators?
MLK, Kennedy? Einstein, the Bomb – '70s indicators?
Wobbly frame (full of tentative hints, brush-strokes).
Someone's touching my piano. Fingers plumb the keys.
I am walking through the forest, Lena... Mira; I am
sensing showy lady-slippers... *cypripedia reginae*. Hmm.
These oceantides of memory will bring you to your knees.

Let's follow the mouthtrail, beaded with seeds.
Around Great Auk Mountain, along the shore
to Whitsuntide – where the clans gather
by 52 sarcens, for each of 12 high meeds.
The wake of the red-haired coracle led back
to Narragansett Bay, where we found our *Son
of Rose*, lapped in funereal cedar – that broken
boy-o, taken from Dallas on a plane. Heartcrack.

My tinny mechanical woodpecker knock-knocks
upon his Lincoln-log toy cabin. This Byzantium
victrola, frail as a faded valentine – knicknack,
memento from somebody's Iowa drawing-room
– 19th-century, maybe. In the Twin Cities
the twins take turns, appeasing appearances;
nobody wants a scapegoat tipping over niceties
we work so hard to enjoy! My Dad's copies

of his grandfather's – Judge Hale's – Elizabethan
Magna Carta (*Tottel's, London*). Who gave
their last tin cup... *les soldats inconnus*, each one.

With malice toward none, with charity for all. Brave
lighthouse in the Bay, outlasting hurricanes –
keeping standing up out there, to light the way.
In memory, of memory, for memory. Green pines
my mother tiled around a mirror... none shall betray.

I am a double-dealer, with a double soul... a wavering
unruly Gemini, Granddad. Weak-minded fool. & yet
is it not the desolate climax of *King Lear* – transmuting
suddenly to seraphic lightness (birds caught in a net,
piping blithe childish innocent spirit) – sepulchral root
of that strange marvelous grace of his last, gentle plays?
Natasha, Nadezhda... limp along on my dusty route,
arm-in-arm with me; we bear the cusp of better days.

*

Equality, union, connection. A murmur of wasps
around the oak-bole, their red-buzzing gall.
My mother etched a plain backdoor, orthogonal.
Far *509 Arthur*, in Mendelssohn. Twin iron hasps.

It was a miniature traveling stone. Old King Henry,
ready to retire to his chamber (in Jerusalem)...

Prince Hal will crown himself (briefly, shamefacedly).

Boy in green cloak sheds tears of glee – bees hum.
Planet's Restoration Day? *What will be will be.*

Bright-black Penny – strong arms of Elena Shvarts...
hold me up, lift me. My feeble legs are giving out.
Sally, Francesca, Phoebe, & Sophie... *c'est tout.*
Les jeux sont faits. Your mercy's all my arts.

334

My father's ashes lie five steps from here
under a big red pine, on a cliff by the lake.
My brother's building a primitive monument –
a simple pyramid, held in place with concrete.
My circling poem tries to hold things dear
in a similar way – meek fumblings we make
that bring to mind our evanescence, *Paraclete*.
O seraph-advocate, hum your consoling argument!

Some pour out their lives among trials, thorns –
Sargasso Seas of dubious entanglement; the seagulls'
quarrels, crying over salt – the combers' thundering
against encrusted ribs of wrecks. Coke (Sir Edward)
steered the common law as best he could, toward
disinterested equity – primordial right no scorn
of the servile minions of power ever actually annuls.
Man labors at a blessed round, despite all plundering.

Who is the judge, who gives her life in service
to the common good? From natural, abundant love
& compassion, clear as children in the playground –
tending to laughter & delight in each other's joy?
Who is that martyr – like Boethius – for civilization,
taken away by brute storms of arrogant injustice –
yet leaving behind a scent of well-being? No ploy
of malice can dissipate such goodness from above.

I am here, father, beside your woodland grave,
in the melodious splendor of the first day of July.
Phoebes, robins chant & warble their sad-happy
melodies, improvise into the green conclave.
You loved it here; you knew how to tap the sappy
& laborious wisdom required to abide here, by & by.

335

The pine-scent & the shadows of upright trees
extend from unseen Kings & Lincolns in this paradise.

The silence of these woodlands renders tacit
judgement on the blaring of our public sphere;
it finds its echo in pure adoration of the human
soul, that heart uplifted through the high blue air
to the eagle-eyrie of an omnipresent *Paraclete* –
Spirit proceeding from the embodied *Child of Woman*
& *Son of Man*, & from the One beyond our numbering;
Equality Who is *Union*, *Connection* – beyond all
       wondering.

To the west of the Isle of Mull, across the strait
by the Three Sisters in Kilkenny, over river Barrow
the *Rose Kennedy Bridge* spans, peacefully, in memory
of her son, JFK. The silky threads of summer's Fate
knot there in glittering sea-sunlight; through sorrow
& joy, the continuum of an endless round will play,
& we will remember that *eyre* of ancient kings
gathered to right the coracle of every *Thing* (all things).

Blithe sails crisscross Newport Harbor. The dream
of Narragansett summer settles in your bones, sighing.
The young prince drowses on skiff-planks, beam –
reads a Shakespeare play. Hamlet, almost dying
in London, runs a switcheroo with his father's seal;
that covenant within his heart was sealed with wax
& blood. *Come about*! – tyranny's usurpation to repeal.
So, for the rightful heir, the times sharpen their axe.

Ineffable & interplanetary grace floats like the wind
beyond our ken, beyond the stars & galaxies.
The shepherd of shepherds comes in child-disguise,

336

like *Sophia* dancing – leaping for the sluggish tribes
of nervous, over-burdened humankind. & she will bind
their wounded rivals, all their fractious scribes
within one contrapuntal dissonance of inequalities;
a tuneful Restoration chord, her melody of melodies.

George Berkeley, in his eyrie there near Newport,
looks out toward the sea of a summer morning.
Awaits his *Royal Oak*; dreams of his mowers
rowing across the azure to Bermuda. Sensing
divine *Shekinah*, he tingles with a fine transport
to fellowship of Paradise – all those blissful glowers.
He notes that firm, wave-washed Rose Island Light;
his heart hums, filled with *Agape*... her oceanic might.

6.27–7.1.22

337